Inhalt

1 Caring for People
- The balloon debate 6
- A homemaker – who, me? 7
- Care workers and their jobs 9
- Vocabulary 12

2 Growing up
- What is a family? 14
- Typical teenager! 16
- Between two worlds 18
- Child abuse 20
- Vocabulary 22

3 Getting old
- Some facts and figures 24
- The third age 26
- Difficult decisions 28
- Caring for older people 30
- Vocabulary 32

4 Everyone is a person
- Damita's accident 34
- Down's Syndrome 36
- Caring for the homeless 38
- The Samaritans 40
- Vocabulary 42

5 A home of your own
- My place 44
- Who does what at home? 46
- Safety in the home 48
- A dream kitchen 50
- Vocabulary 52

Inhalt

6 Staying healthy
A healthy diet 54
The work of a dietician 56
Alcohol 58
'E' is for Ecstasy 60
Vocabulary 62

7 Shop till you drop
Your household budget 64
What kind of shopper are you? 66
Know your rights 68
Advertising 70
Vocabulary 72

8 Caring for the environment
The world in which we live 74
The environment and your home 76
Helping others to understand 78
A different kind of care worker 80
Vocabulary 82

Wordfields
A Care workers and their jobs 84
B People and relationships 86
C Health 88
D The home 90
E Money and shopping 92
F The environment 94

Vorwort

Caring for People New Edition ist ein neu entwickelter Baustein für Englisch-Lernende in hauswirtschaftlichen und sozialpädagogischen Berufsfeldern. Das Werk ergänzt *Keep Going 1 Neue Ausgabe* (Best.-Nr. 24245), auf das der Wortschatz abgestimmt ist, kann jedoch auch als Ergänzung zu anderen Lehrwerken, die auf den Abschluss der Mittleren Reife hinführen, genutzt werden. Möchten Lernende aus dem Bereich der Pflegeberufe ihre Englischkenntnisse erweitern, finden sie in *Caring for People New Edition* einen mehr als nützlichen Begleiter.

Caring for People New Edition besteht aus acht Einheiten (Units), von denen vier den sozialpflegerischen und drei den hauswirtschaftlichen Berufen gewidmet sind. Die letzte Unit rundet das Thema ab, da es 'Caring', als unser aller Sorge für die Umwelt darstellt.

Caring for People New Edition bietet den Lernenden eine große Bandbreite an Themen: die hauswirtschaftliche Organisation, die gesunde Ernährung, die Fürsorge für jüngere und ältere Menschen, der Umgang mit Drogenabhängigen, das Leben mit Behinderten und manchem mehr. Vermittelt werden diese informativen, vielseitigen Themen in Erfahrungsberichten, Fachtexten, Tagebuchauszügen, Interviews mit 'care workers' und Krankenschwestern und Zeitungsberichten – alles in allem eine Zusammensetzung, die aktuell berufsbezogen zum Lernen motiviert.

Sowohl die Units wie auch die Texte können in beliebiger Reihenfolge durchgearbeitet werden. Begünstigt wird dies durch das griffige Doppelseitenprinzip, bei dem ein Thema auf zwei gegenüberliegenden Seiten inhaltlich kompakt behandelt wird. Aufgrund dessen kann *Caring for People New Edition* im Unterricht nach Wunsch als Ergänzung im Wechselspiel mit *Keep Going 1 Neue Ausgabe* eingesetzt werden. Die entsprechend flexible Übungsgestaltung ermöglicht es, die Units oder einzelne Aufgaben, selbständig in Einzel-, Partner- oder Gruppenarbeit oder gemeinsam mit dem Lehrer/der Lehrerin zu bearbeiten. Die optisch ansprechenden Illustrationen und Fotos, die das Wesentliche der Texte auf- oder einen besonders interessanten Aspekt herausgreifen, sind ebenso humorig wie abwechslungsreich.

Caring for People New Edition enthält Übungen, die stringent didaktisch aufeinander abgestimmt sind:

- 'Before reading' bereitet auf die Übung vor, 'While reading' begleitet das Lesen des Textes und 'After reading' überprüft mit Hilfe von Fragen, ob der Text verstanden wurde.
- Die 'Talking and doing'-Übungen sind handlungsorientiert und regen zu Diskussionen in kleinen Gruppen, zu selbständigen Schreibübungen oder anderen spachlichen Aktiväten in Partner- oder Gruppenarbeit an, indem sie den Inhalt des Textes noch einmal aufgreifen.
- Mit Hilfe der 'Revision spots' wird die in der Unit behandelte Grammatik wiederholt und deren Kenntnis mit Hilfe einer Übung gefestigt. Alle Übungen lassen die Lernenden ihren Fachwortschatz sorgfältig und umfassend erweitern und in abwechslungsreichen Wortschatzübungen erproben.

Caring for People New Edition ist ein Werk, das Lernende anregt, aktiv auf Englisch am sprachlichen Geschehen teilzunehmen. Eine Wortschatzliste mit dem entsprechenden Fachwortschatz schließt jede Unit ab und am Schluss wird das Lehrwerk mit sechs Wortfeldlisten abgerundet, so dass der Benutzer des Buches rasch auf das relevante Fachvokabular zurückgreifen kann.

Caring for People New Edition ist ein für die pflegerische Arbeit geschriebenes Lehrwerk, das die facettenreichen Aspekte dieses Berufsfeldes praxisnah in gängigem Englisch gestalterisch anspruchsvoll vermittelt. Wir wünschen den Lernenden viel Vergnügen, wenn sie sich über ihre beruflichen Erfahrungen und Kenntnisse lebhaft auf Englisch austauschen.

Der Autor

1 Caring for people

The balloon debate

High above the earth, five people are in a balloon. Unfortunately, together they are too heavy: one must jump out. But which one? Naturally, they all think that they – and their jobs – are so important that they should stay in the balloon. The farmer explains that he is important because he produces food. The police officer, the factory manager and the artist give their reasons.

Finally, there is one other person in the balloon, too. This is what she says:

'I care for people. I am the mother, father and partner who makes the home in which you live and your children grow up. I am the nurse, the social worker and the helper who is there when you need me, when perhaps things in your life are going wrong. Without me, the world would be an empty, cold and unfriendly place. I cannot jump out. I *must* stay in the balloon!'

After reading

1 Answer these questions on the text.

 a Why do the people in the balloon want to show that they are all important?
 b What does the farmer say?
 c What do you think the police officer, the factory manager and the artist say?
 d Who speaks last?

2 Farmers produce food. What do these people do?

 a teachers
 b doctors
 c reporters
 d builders
 e chefs
 f engineers

Talking and doing

3 'Caring for people' can mean being a 'homemaker' or a professional like a nurse or a social worker. Which job do you want to do? Why?

Caring for people   Unit 1

A homemaker – who, me?

Being a 'homemaker' – a parent, housewife (or househusband) – may seem a long way in the future when you are still young, but you probably have some ideas about it already.

Talking and doing

1 Talk about these pictures.

2 In a group answer these questions and talk about getting married.

    a Do you want to get married one day?
    b What is the best age to get married?
    c Is it better to live with someone for a while before you get married to them?
    d Is it necessary to get married at all? Is it not better just to live with a partner?

3 In the same group, discuss having children.

    a Do you want to have children?
    b What is a 'good' number of children to have?
    c Does it matter to you if they are boys or girls?
    d What is the best age to become a parent?

Unit 1   Caring for people

4 Now talk about 'home' with the other students in your group.

    a   Do you want to live in the town or village where you live now, or would you prefer to move to another place?
    b   What is your 'ideal' flat or house like?
    c   Do you like shopping and housework?
    d   Would you be a good homemaker?

Revision spot

How to ask for and give an opinion

What do you think about …?
Do you believe that …?
What about …?

I think (that) …
I don't think that …
I believe that …
It seems to me that …
I would say that …
Well, in my opinion …

Agreeing and disagreeing

I agree.
I think so, too.
I think you're absolutely right (about that).

Sorry, I don't agree with you.
Sorry, I don't think so at all.
You must be joking!

Practice

These two letters appeared in the July and August editions of a young people's magazine. What are the missing words?

Dear Tony

My new boyfriend is a lovely guy but he looks at other girls all the time! However, I don't want to be the jealous type so I don't say anything.

I (1) ✱✱✱ it's important that you trust your partner. In my (2) ✱✱✱ too many girls want to 'own' their boyfriend and that's wrong. My friends (3) ✱✱✱ I'm stupid. (4) ✱✱✱ do you think about this?

Dear Tony

I read the letter in last month's magazine from the girl whose boyfriend looks at other girls and I just laughed! I (5) ✱✱✱ with all her friends – she must be crazy.

It (6) ✱✱✱ to me that if you are going out with someone you should look at them and not every other girl in the room! Your answer to her letter told her to find a new boy. I think you're (7) ✱✱✱ right!

Care workers and their jobs

> The professionals who care for people are called 'care workers'. Here are three, and their very different jobs.

While reading **1** Copy this table and fill it in as you read the texts. If you wish, you can work with two partners: each of you can fill in the table for one of the care workers, then tell the others about him or her.

Care workers' jobs

Name	Job	What he or she did before	Why he or she likes the job
1	× × ×	× × ×	× × ×
2	× × ×	× × ×	× × ×
3	× × ×	× × ×	× × ×

Susie Norris – Community Nurse

Community nurses are nurses who visit people in their homes. They also go to kindergartens, and run clinics, for example for young mothers – or women who are going to become mothers (ante-natal clinics).

5 " It is a busy job, but I like it because I am free to organize my own work. I worked in a hospital before I became a community nurse, and I prefer this job.

Community nurses visit people in their homes.

It is important to be well-organized!
10 Many people living at home – older people, for example – like to see me regularly, and I need time
15 to talk to them.

Perhaps the most important thing about the job is being able to talk to
20 people easily. I meet all sorts of different people every day: you have to get on well with all of them. "

Mary Layland – working with blind people

Mary helps blind students do everyday jobs like cooking, washing and going to town.

"I work at a college for blind people. I run a hostel where five of the students live – I'm the 'hostel warden'. I wake them up in the morning and help with washing and dressing, then take some of them to their lessons. In the afternoons and evenings we cook and eat together, and learn how to do everyday jobs like washing clothes or shopping.

I began here first as a volunteer, then went to college for two years, and came back full-time.

I really love the job: I feel that I am doing something useful. You have to be very patient, and have a sense of humour. But the students are all great. I think the most important thing is that you remember that they don't want you to do everything for them – they want to learn to do things for themselves. It is the same for everyone who is disabled, I think they are people first, and disabled second."

Malik Asubar – Youth Worker

"I work with young people in the inner-city. It's not a particularly nice place for the kids to grow up: there's a lot of crime, and not much for the young people to do. So, sports and clubs are much better for them than just standing around on the streets.

There are four of us in the team. Together, we run a youth club, sports teams, and classes in the evenings in English, maths and computers. A lot of the kids don't like school much and the classes may help them to get jobs.

One of the most important things about the job is being able to work in a team with other people. You also need lots of energy!"

Caring for people   Unit 1

The job is great. I'm Asian myself, and I really feel I'm helping the
95 black and Asian kids who live here. Before I started here I worked in an office. This
100 is much better!"

There is often not much for people to do in inner cities. Sports and clubs are much better than just standing around on the streets.

After reading

2   Explain these parts of the text in your own words.

a   I am free to organize my own work (lines 5–6)
b   you have to get on well with all of them (lines 23–24)
c   I began here first as a volunteer (lines 38–40)
d   they are people first and disabled second (lines 62–63)
e   the inner-city (line 65)
f   sports and clubs are much better for them than just standing around on the streets (lines 70–73)

Talking and doing

3   What makes a good care worker? Look at the three texts and in a group make a list of what the people say they need in their jobs or have to be able to do in them. Then try to write down one or two other things which you think of yourself which make a good care worker.

Example: Care workers need to be well-organized.

> **Useful expressions**
>
> Care workers need to/must …
> They have to be able to …
> In care work it is important to …
> The most important thing about … is (that) …

4   Do you want to be a professional care worker? Find out what the job is called in English. Write three or four sentences about the job and read them to the class.

11

Unit 1

Vocabulary

Zeichenerklärung: ⚠ Achtung   ◆▶ Gegenteil   ≈ (ungefähr) gleichbedeutend mit

to care for	[ˈkeə fə]	versorgen, sorgen für
		≈ **to look after**
balloon debate	[bəˈluːn dɪbeɪt]	Ballon Debatte (Gesellschaftsspiel)
unfortunately	[ʌnˈfɔːtʃənətli]	leider
heavy	[ˈhevi]	schwer
		◆▶ **light** – leicht
to explain	[ɪkˈspleɪn]	erklären
artist	[ˈɑːtɪst]	Künstler/in
finally	[ˈfaɪnəli]	schließlich
		≈ **at last**
to grow up	[ˌɡrəʊ ˈʌp]	aufwachsen
		⚠ unregelmäßig
		I grew up on a farm.
helper	[ˈhelpə]	Helfer/in
perhaps	[pəˈhæps]	vielleicht
unfriendly	[ʌnˈfrendli]	unfreundlich
		⚠ Adverb: **in an unfriendly way**
builder	[ˈbɪldə]	Bauarbeiter
chef	[ʃef]	Koch
		⚠ **boss** – Chef/in
engineer	[ˌendʒɪˈnɪə]	Ingenieur/in
homemaker	[ˈhəʊmmeɪkə]	jemand, der ein Haus gemütlich macht
housewife	[ˈhaʊswaɪf]	Hausfrau
		Plural: **housewives**
househusband	[ˈhaʊshʌzbənd]	Hausmann
to get married (to someone)	[get ˈmærɪd tə]	jdn heiraten
		⚠ unregelmäßig
		She got married last week.
does it matter?	[dʌz ɪt ˈmætə]	spielt es eine Rolle?
ideal	[aɪˈdɪəl]	ideal
		⚠ Aussprache
housework	[ˈhaʊswɜːk]	Hausarbeit
		⚠ **homework** – Hausaufgabe
to disagree (with)	[ˌdɪsəˈɡriː]	nicht einverstanden sein
		◆▶ **agree** – zustimmen
you must be joking	[ju ˌmʌst bi ˈdʒəʊkɪŋ]	Du machst Witze!
to appear	[əˈpɪə]	erscheinen
lovely guy	[ˈlʌvli ɡaɪ]	ein lieber Kerl
however	[haʊˈevə]	jedoch
the jealous type	[ðə ˈdʒeləs taɪp]	der eifersüchtige Typ
		≈ **possessive** – besitzergreifend
to trust	[trʌst]	vertrauen
		◆▶ **mistrust/distrust** – misstrauen

Vocabulary — Unit 1

whose	[huːz]	*dessen*
to go out (with someone)	[ˌgəʊ ˈaʊt wɪð]	*gehen mit* ⚠ *unregelmäßig* **I've been going out with my boyfriend for two years.**
care worker	[ˈkeə wɜːkə]	*Pfleger/in*
professional	[prəˈfeʃnl]	*Spezialist/in*
community	[kəˈmjuːnəti]	*Gemeinde*
community nurse	[kəˈmjuːnəti nɜːs]	*Gemeindeschwester*
to run	[rʌn]	*leiten* ⚠ *unregelmäßig* **She ran her own business for ten years.**
clinic	[ˈklɪnɪk]	*Klinik*
ante-natal clinic	[ˌæntiˈneɪtl klɪnɪk]	*Geburtsklinik*
regularly	[ˈregjələli]	*regelmäßig* ◄► **irregularly**
easily	[ˈiːzəli]	*leicht*
to get on (well) with someone	[ˌget ɒn ˈwel wɪð]	*mit jdm gut auskommen* ⚠ *unregelmäßig* **I get on very well with her.**
blind	[blaɪnd]	*blind* ⚠ *Aussprache*
hostel	[ˈhɒstl]	*Wohnheim*
hostel warden	[ˈhɒstl wɔːdn]	*Wohnheimleiter/in*
to wake (someone up)	[ˌweɪk ˈʌp]	*jdn aufwecken* ⚠ *unregelmäßig* **He woke me up early.**
to dress	[dres]	*(sich) anziehen*
volunteer	[ˌvɒlənˈtɪə]	*Freiwillige/r* vgl. Adjektiv: **voluntary** – *freiwillig*
patient	[ˈpeɪʃnt]	*geduldig* ◄► **impatient** – *ungeduldig*
sense of humour	[ˌsens əv ˈhjuːmə]	*Sinn für Humor* **He has no ~.**
disabled	[dɪsˈeɪbld]	*behindert*
youth worker	[ˈjuːθ wɜːkə]	*Sozialarbeiter/in für Jugendliche*
inner-city	[ˌɪnəˈsɪti]	*Innenstadt-*
particularly	[pəˈtɪkjələli]	*besonders* ≈ **especially**
kid (Umgangssprache)	[kɪd]	*Kind*
youth club	[ˈjuːθ klʌb]	*Jugendklub*
team	[tiːm]	*Mannschaft*
maths	[mæθs]	*Mathe(matik)*
Asian	[ˈeɪʃn]	*asiatisch (hier: von indischer Abstammung)*
to stand around on the streets	[ˌstænd əraʊnd ɒn ðə ˈstriːt]	*in den Straßen herumlungern* ⚠ *unregelmäßig*
expression	[ɪkˈspreʃn]	*Ausdruck* Auch: *Gesichtsausdruck*

2 Growing up

What is a family?

A family is the place where most of us grow up. It is where we learn about the world, and become the people that we are. But what is a family? Care workers have tried to define the main types.

While reading   **1**   Find which text (A–D) goes with which picture (1–4).

A   *The nuclear family*
For many years, most people's idea of a 'normal' family has been the so-called nuclear family: mum, dad, and one or more kids. There are probably relatives like aunts, uncles and grandparents, but they do not live in the same house. In the very traditional nuclear family, mum often stayed at home and dad went out to work. In recent years, the number of nuclear families has declined. In fact today only about fifty per cent of families are still like this.

B *The single-parent family*
Single-parent families are those where there is only one parent, either a father, or more often a mother. This can happen when one of the parents dies, or when they get divorced, or never get married. Today, some women prefer to bring up their children without a partner – as a single mother. The number of these families has increased and now about one in five of all families are single-parent families.

C *The extended family*
In many parts of the world the extended family is the normal type – and there are lots of families like this in Europe, too. 'Extended family' just means that the group which lives together is larger than mum, dad and the kids – it includes grandparents, for example, or aunts and uncles (and maybe their children).

D *The reconstituted or stepfamily*
Stepfamilies happen when two people come together who were married before. One or both of them may have children already, – and they can, of course, have more children together. So in one house there may be a natural mother or a natural father, a stepmother or a stepfather, children, stepchildren, brothers, sisters and stepbrothers and stepsisters. As the number of people getting divorced increases, we will probably see more and more stepfamilies in the future.

After reading

2 For each sentence, find a word or expression in the text which means the opposite of the word or expression which is underlined.

Example: Single-parent families are usually smaller than nuclear families, but extended families are normally *larger*.

a Many years ago almost all families were nuclear families. ✱✱✱, however, the number of this type of family has declined.
b Of all the people who get married, about one in three in Europe now ✱✱✱ later.
c The number of nuclear families has declined in Europe, but the number of single-parent and stepfamilies has ✱✱✱.
d Men who get married to more than one woman may seem strange or unusual to us in Europe, but in some countries it is quite ✱✱✱.
e Fewer and fewer people in Europe now have a very large number of children. ✱✱✱ have only one child, or perhaps no children at all.

Talking and doing

3 Talk about these ideas in a group, then tell the class your ideas.

a Make a list of all the different ways in which family life (in Europe) is changing. Use the text and add ideas of your own.
b The text describes four different types of family. Are there others?
c Care workers believe that children can be happy in many different types of family. Do you agree with this? Do you think that one type of family is better than another? What are the advantages and disadvantages for the child of each of the four types which are described above?

Unit 2 Growing up

Typical teenager!

Gina is 16 and lives with her mother. She often calls her a 'typical teenager' – Gina, of course, often calls her mum a 'typical mother'!

While reading 1 What do you think? Copy and fill in this table, then say if Gina or her mother is 'right' about each thing.

	Gina thinks …	Her mother thinks …
Gina's room	× × ×	× × ×
School	× × ×	× × ×
Helping in the home	× × ×	× × ×

Gina says …

'Mum and dad got divorced four years ago, and I chose to live with mum. Mum is great, and we get on well together. The only problem is that she still thinks I'm a kid!

Her big thing is my room. I know it's a bit of a mess sometimes, but it is my room and that's how I like it. If she wants it to be clean, then she can clean it herself – I'm quite happy in it!

Homework is another problem. I do my homework, but she wants me to do it every evening at the same time. She seems to think that if I don't have 'a system' (as she calls it), I won't do it. I think I have to learn to organize my life myself. My marks at school are OK (I think).

Mum has a job and is busy all day. She thinks I should help in the house. But I'm busy, too, and I don't see why I should. She doesn't have to work – and anyway, mums are supposed to cook, aren't they?'

Growing up — Unit 2

Gina's mother says …

'Life has not been easy since my husband left four years ago, but it's great that I have Gina and she seems quite happy, which is the important thing. The trouble is she is so lazy! You should see her room! It looks terrible and she refuses to clean it herself.

School is sometimes a problem, too. I try to get Gina to do her homework regularly, but she always seems to find the TV, or her friends more interesting and sometimes I don't think she does it at all. This year, her marks at school are a lot worse than they were last year.

I also think she could help more in the house. I work hard to get money so that we can live well, and I'm often tired when I get home. It would be really nice if just sometimes Gina cooked a meal!'

Talking and doing

2 Cleaning bedrooms and homework are fairly typical problems between teenagers and parents. With a partner, make list of other problems which you can think of.

3 Is it really difficult being a teenager? Why (not)?

4 This is a letter from a parent to a magazine. You are the magazine's 'expert'. Work in a group. Write a short reply giving some helpful ideas.

She costs us a FORTUNE!

Our 14-year-old daughter is always on the phone. I have spoken to her about it, but she can't seem to understand why I get angry and there have been lots of arguments between us.

It is mostly friends from school that she talks to – sometimes for hours – people that she has seen all day and will see again tomorrow.

I don't want to be a difficult parent, but all this phoning is costing a fortune. What can I do?

Unit 2 Growing up

Between two worlds

Many thousands of people from India and Pakistan came to live in Britain in the 1960s. For their children – who were born in Britain – there is sometimes a special problem about growing up. This is one girl's story.

Before reading **1** Look at the title above and write down what you think the problem is.

'Don't misunderstand me – I love my parents and I know my father only wants the best for me. But sometimes I feel like two different people and it is not easy.

At home I am the obedient daughter who always does what my parents tell me to. But once I leave the house I am a 'normal' British teenager who wants to go to parties and discos and be with other young people. I hate doing it, but sometimes I lie to my parents about where I'm going. I even hide clothes in my room to wear when I go out.

Things are not so bad for my brother. He has more freedom than me. But Asian parents are very strict with their daughters.

The biggest problem is boys. My parents don't want me to see English boys at all, not even as friends, and I'm not supposed to be alone with one. But there are some that I like a lot, and I'm really afraid of what will happen if I meet one and fall in love. I know it would break my parents' hearts and cause scandal in our family. It is something that I worry about a lot.

Luckily, I have lots of Asian friends, too, who are in the same situation. We can understand that our parents want us to live in a way that they think is right. They are the ideas that they have had all their lives and it is difficult to change. But we want them to see that we have grown up in Britain, and things are different here. We cannot live between two worlds.'

Growing up Unit 2

After reading 2 Answer these questions about the text.

a Do you think that Raj loves her parents and that they love her?
b How is Raj different at home and outside home?
c Give an example of how being 'two people' can be very difficult.
d Do Asian boys have the same problems as Asian girls. Why (not)?
e What is the thing that Raj is most afraid will happen in the future? How would her family feel about this if it happened?
f What makes Raj's life a little easier?
g What, according to Raj, must Asian parents try to understand?

Talking and doing 3 Now find a good headline for each paragraph in Raj's story. The first one could be 'I love my parents but …'.

4 Work in a small group. You are a team of care workers who often work with Asian families. Today, you have a meeting with some parents and some young Asian boys and girls. You want to help them with their problems. What will you say to the parents? What will you say to their children? What could all of them do to make their situation better?

Revision spot

have to/must, must not, don't have to/needn't

Raj **has to/must be** a good 'Asian' daughter at home. (= *muss*)
She **must not be** alone with English boys. (= *darf nicht*)
Her English friends **don't have to/needn't worry** about the same problems (= *müssen nicht/brauchen nicht*)

Practice Complete these sentences about Raj using *have to/must, must not*, or *don't have to/needn't*.

a Asian parents are often very strict with their daughters. At home, Raj (1) ✱✱✱ wear traditional clothes and help her mother in the kitchen. She also often (2) ✱✱✱ look after her younger brothers and sisters.
b On the other hand, she (3) ✱✱✱ smoke or drink alcohol.
c Because he is a boy, her brother Rakesh (4) ✱✱✱ help with the housework or look after the children: men (5) ✱✱✱ do this kind of work.
d When she goes out, Raj is suddenly with English teenagers and she (6) ✱✱✱ adapt and become a different person.
e She likes to wear different clothes when she is out. Her parents would not like these, so she (7) ✱✱✱ hide them in her room.
f English girls (8) ✱✱✱ worry about falling in love with English boys. But Raj (9) ✱✱✱ think about this: her parents want her to marry an Asian boy.
g In my opinion, Asian parents (10) ✱✱✱ understand that their children have grown up in a different culture, even if it is hard for them to do so.

Child abuse

Tragically, thousands of children are abused each year, most often in their own families. There are many different forms of child abuse. This text shows one of them. It is a letter from a young girl to an organization which helps abused children.

My name is Lucy and I am 10 years old. it is Saterday and I am in the house on my own ecept for my cat. I and she are lonely in the one room. please can you write to me and mark it private to this address.

After reading 1 Lucy is a 'home alone' child – her parents often leave her for a long time while they go out. With a partner, write a short paragraph about Lucy's life. Think about the things below.

    a Who are her parents?
    b Why do they leave her alone?
    c What other things do they perhaps not do for her?
    d How do you think Lucy feels?
    e What does she do, eat, etc while her parents are out?
    f What could happen to her while she is alone?

Talking and doing 2 Ray Matthews is a Child Protection Worker. Recently a reporter for a magazine for professional care workers wrote an article about Ray and his job. Read the article and with a partner make a list of the questions that you think the reporter asked him. Then practise the interview.

Example: Is child abuse a new problem?

Job profile

This week we talk to Ray Matthews, who is part of the care team at Addenbrooks Hospital in Cambridge. Ray is a ...

Child Protection Worker

We seem to read more and more in the papers nowadays about child abuse but, according to Ray Matthews, it is not a new problem. Parents, he says, have always beaten their children or sent them to work for long hours in factories. But no one talked about it then. It is only in recent years that we have started to think about the problem and to realise just how many abused children there are. And there are more than we think, more than those few cases we all read about in the newspapers.

Ray sees many sorts of problems in his work: physical abuse, sexual abuse, and 'home alone' children, for example. The children are of all ages, from babies to teenagers. Many of the people that Ray works with are teenagers who have run away from home because of abuse.

Ray explains that there are a number of different reasons for child abuse. Poor living conditions are one – it can be very hard to be with a small child all the time in a tiny flat. Sometimes parents are too young to know how to look after a child. Or again, stepfamilies can be a problem where, say, the stepfather does not accept his partner's children. But most often, the problem is that the parents need help themselves – many are aggressive people because they were once abused children themselves.

Ray Matthews has been a Child Protection Worker now for just over a year. He is not sure yet how he finds the work. Sometimes, he says, it is very shocking and he wants to stop. But he also feels that he is doing something that really helps and that makes him want to carry on.

Unit 2

Vocabulary

Zeichenerklärung: ⚠ Achtung ◀▶ Gegenteil ≈ (ungefähr) gleichbedeutend mit

to define	[dɪˈfaɪn]	*definieren*
the main types	[ðə meɪn taɪps]	*Hauptarten*
nuclear family	[ˌnjuːkliə ˈfæməli]	*Kernfamilie*
relative	[ˈrelətɪv]	*Verwandte/r*
		vgl. Adjektiv: **related** – *verwandt*
in recent years	[ɪn ˈriːsnt jɪəz]	*in den letzten Jahren*
to decline	[dɪˈklaɪn]	*fallen*
in fact	[ɪn ˈfækt]	*tatsächlich*
single-parent	[ˌsɪŋgl peərənt]	*Alleinerziehende/r*
to get divorced	[get dɪˈvɔːst]	*sich scheiden lassen*
		⚠ unregelmäßig
extended family	[ɪkˌstendɪd ˈfæməli]	*Großfamilie*
to include	[ɪnˈkluːd]	*einbeziehen*
		◀▶ **to leave out** – *auslassen*
reconstituted family	[ˌriːˈkɒnstɪtjuːtɪd fæməli]	*eine Familie, die aus mehreren schon existierenden Familien besteht*
stepfamily(-ies)	[ˈstepfæməli]	*Stieffamilie*
		ebenso: **stepmother** usw.
natural mother	[ˌnætʃrəl ˈmʌðə]	*biologische Mutter*
step-	[step]	*Stief-*
to increase	[ɪnˈkriːs]	*zunehmen* ◀▶ **to decrease**
underlined	[ˌʌndəˈlaɪnd]	*unterstrichen*
almost	[ˈɔːlməʊst]	*fast*
		≈ **nearly**
later	[ˈleɪtə]	*später*
strange	[streɪndʒ]	*seltsam* ⚠ Aussprache
perhaps	[pəˈhæps]	*vielleicht*
to add	[æd]	*hinzufügen*
typical	[ˈtɪpɪkl]	*typisch*
a bit of a mess	[ə ˌbɪt əv ə ˈmes]	*ein bißchen unordentlich*
system	[ˈsɪstəm]	*System* ⚠ Aussprache
mark	[mɑːk]	*Note*
to be supposed to	[bi səˈpəʊzd tə]	*etw tun sollen* ⚠ unregelmäßig
lazy	[ˈleɪzi]	*faul*
to refuse	[rɪˈfjuːz]	*sich weigern*
		vgl. Nomen: **refusal** – *Weigerung*
meal	[miːl]	*Essen*
helpful	[ˈhelpfl]	*hilfreich*
fortune	[ˈfɔːtʃuːn]	*Vermögen*
she is always on the phone	[ʃiːz ˌɔːlweɪz ɒn ðə ˈfəʊn]	*sie telefoniert dauernd*
argument	[ˈɑːgjumənt]	*Streit*
mostly	[ˈməʊstli]	*hauptsächlich*
		≈ **usually, normally**

to phone	[fəʊn]	anrufen
special	['speʃl]	besondere/r
to misunderstand	[ˌmɪsʌndə'stænd]	missverstehen △ unregelmäßig
		She misunderstood me.
obedient	[ə'biːdiənt]	gehorsam
		◄► **disobedient** – ungehorsam
to lie	[laɪ]	lügen
		vgl. Nomen: **liar** – Lügner/in
to hide	[haɪd]	verstecken △ unregelmäßig
freedom	['friːdəm]	Freiheit
strict	[strɪkt]	streng
to fall in love	[fɔːl ɪn 'lʌv wɪð]	sich in jdn verlieben
(with someone)		△ unregelmäßig
to break someone's	[breɪk sʌmwʌnz 'hɑːt]	jdm das Herz brechen
heart		△ unregelmäßig
to cause a scandal	[kɔːz ə 'skændl]	ein Skandal verursachen
headline	['hedlaɪn]	Schlagzeile
paragraph	['pærəgrɑːf]	Absatz
meeting	['miːtɪŋ]	Besprechung
alcohol	['ælkəhɒl]	Alkohol △ Schreibung
suddenly	['sʌdnli]	plötzlich
to adapt	[ə'dæpt]	(sich) anpassen
to marry (someone)	['mæri]	jdn heiraten
culture	['kʌltʃə]	Kultur
child abuse	['tʃaɪld əbjuːs]	Kindesmisshandlung
tragically	['trædʒɪkli]	tragisch
to abuse	[ə'bjuːz]	missbrauchen △ Aussprache
		vgl. Nomen: [əbjuːs]
organization	[ˌɔːgənaɪ'zeɪʃn]	Organisation
Child Protection	[tʃaɪld prə'tekʃn wɜːkə]	Mitarbeiter/in für Kinderschutz
Worker		
recently	['riːsntli]	neulich
article	['ɑːtɪkl]	Artikel △ Aussprache
according to	[ə'kɔːdɪŋ tə]	laut
nowadays	['naʊədeɪz]	heutzutage
to beat	[biːt]	schlagen △ unregelmäßig
to realise	['rɪəlaɪz]	erkennen
physical	['fɪzɪkl]	körperlich
		◄► **mental** – geistig
sexual	['sekʃuəl]	sexuell
living conditions	['lɪvɪŋ kəndɪʃnz]	Wohnverhältnisse
tiny	['taɪni]	winzig
		◄► **huge** [hjuːdʒ]
to accept	[ək'sept]	annehmen
aggressive	[ə'gresɪv]	aggressiv △ Aussprache
sure	[ʃʊə]	sicher
shocking	['ʃɒkɪŋ]	schockierend
to carry on (doing	[ˌkæri 'ɒn]	fortfahren (etw zu tun)
something)		

3 Getting old

Some facts and figures

* Is this you in sixty years' time?
* Our image of older people is often quite
* negative – bad-tempered, difficult,
* forgetful ... But don't you get angry
* sometimes and forget things too?

Before reading   **1** What do you think about 'getting old'? With a partner, write down two things.

We are all going to get old – you, me, Tom Cruise. We, however, will live much longer than people did in the past.
5 A man born now can expect to live for about 75 years, a woman for nearly 80.
In 1931 it was only 58 years for men and 62 years for women.
10 Even in 1961, it was 68 years and 74 years.

Women, of course, live longer than men. 49% of the total population are men, but of the people between 65 and 79, 44% are men (56% women),
15 and of those over 80, 70% are women and only 30% men.

More and more people, therefore, are living longer. In 1961, 12% of the population were over 65; in 1981 it was 15% and in 1991 16%. By the year 2021 it will be almost 20%.

Many politicians and others are worried by the growing number of older
20 people in our society. Older people need more nurses, doctors, medicines and hospitals than younger ones. And who will pay their pensions?
In the future, younger people who work may not be able to support the older ones who do not. These are problems which we will need to think and talk about a lot in the coming years.

After reading

2 Copy these tables and complete the statistics. Ask your partner to give you the figures.

Table 1: **How long can you expect to live?**

	1931	1961	Now
Men	58 years	x x x	x x x
Women	x x x	x x x	x x x

Table 2: **Percentage of women and men in the population**

	65-79	80+	Total Population
Men	44%	x x x	x x x
Women	x x x	x x x	x x x

Table 3: **Percentage of older people in the population**

	1961	1981	1991	2021
People over 65	12%	x x x	x x x	x x x

3 True or false? If false, give a true sentence.

a Men live longer than women.
b People live longer now than they did 50 years ago.
c There will be more older people in society in the future.
d Older people do not need as many nurses, doctors or hospitals as younger ones.
e The number of older people in society in the future may be a problem.

4 Look back at your answers to question 3. Can you explain the reasons behind each sentence?

Talking and doing

5 Describe an older person that you know. Who is it? Where do or did you meet him or her? Is he or she forgetful or bad tempered? Does he or she understand young people? Write a short paragraph and read it to the class.

6 In the past, people often worked until they were 60 or 65. Nowadays, many already plan to stop working when they are 50 or 55. How do you feel about this? When do you want to stop working? Why?

Unit 3   Getting old

The third age

We are now beginning to think of the years after retirement as 'the third age' – a time to enjoy!

While reading   **1**   Here are some pages from a magazine for retired people. Read the articles and find which of these headlines belongs to each one.

A   Pedal Power!
B   Advertisements
C   Quiet please – I'm your history teacher

She left school at 14 and as an adult, the most important thing in her life was her family. Now, at 81, Lucy Adamson has started a new life ... she teaches history twice a week in her local community.

When her husband died a few years back, Lucy's life 'stopped'. It was a friend who gave her the idea of starting a history class in the village where she lives. 'My daughter is a history teacher,' she says, 'and I thought she could sit down and help me.' Lucy's daughter, however, didn't agree. She told her mum: 'Go and do it yourself!'.

So she did. Two months later she began the class. 'I've never been so nervous in my life,' says Lucy. 'There were ten people, two of them doctors and one a retired headmaster.' The class all came back the next week – and now Lucy has nearly twenty students. Looking back, she hates to think what would have happened without the class. 'Well I think I know – I would be dead.'

Tom Willis made bicycles for over forty years in a factory. Now he rides them!

'I've always loved bikes,' says Tom, 'and I'm a bit of a fitness fan. So a couple of years ago Jean and I started the Mercury Club with just a few friends.'

The club meets every weekend 'summer and winter'. They visit local places and sometimes a nice pub (or two) – cycling is thirsty work! Tom's next idea is a ride for charity. 'We are going to bike from London to Edinburgh,' he says, 'to raise money for 'Children In Need'. So if you feel like joining us ... ?'

• Holidays •

Roman holiday
Visit Rome with an expert guide. Small friendly groups. Travel and accommodation arranged for you. Tel/Fax Margaret 0039 671428

The Highlands of Scotland
A six-night touring holiday of the north of Scotland, including a talk on the area, a Scottish banquet and traditional Scottish entertainment. Six breakfasts and six dinners. Write now for our brochure to Saga Holidays, Freepost, Folkestone Kent CT20 1BR.

GENERAL

Painting in Spain

Enjoy the spring in Alicante among olives, wild flowers, mountains and beautiful villages.
Bedrooms in family villa. Small classes for artists, non-painting partners welcome.
Ring 01730 814147

French/German/Italian
Language courses all year round at all levels. Small friendly classes. Caledonia Language Courses 20 Eildon Street, Edinburgh
Tel/Fax: 0131 558 7118

After reading 2 Look carefully at the articles again and answer these questions.

    a Who helped her mother by not helping her?
    b Where can you learn to paint in small classes?
    c Who meet every weekend summer and winter?
    d What could Margaret organize for you?
    e Who once made things and now uses one himself?
    f How long is the Saga Holiday?

3 What are the missing words?

    a Lucy teaches history in her local ××× *(Gemeinde)*.
    b One of Lucy's students is a ××× *(pensionierter, ehemaliger)* headmaster.
    c Tom wants to bike from London to Edinburgh to ××× *(aufbringen)* money for 'Children In Need'.
    d On the Roman holiday, the travel and ××× *(Unterkunft)* are arranged for you.
    e If you want to visit Scotland, you should write to Saga Holidays for a ××× *(Prospekt)*.
    f The Caledonia Language School has courses all year round at all ××× *(Niveaus)*.

Talking and doing 4 In your town there is a club for older people. They meet once a week, and like to do new things and meet new people. The club wants to visit your college and talk to your class. Describe what happens. Write a short article about the visit for your college magazine.

Unit 3   Getting old

Difficult decisions

When we get older, it becomes more difficult to do things that were once easy. If we are lucky, there will be someone in our family, or a good friend or neighbour, who can look after us. These people are called 'carers'. However, if there is no one, or the carer is also an older person, there can be some difficult decisions to make.

This is the story of a couple, Stan and Doris Leonard.

Stan and Doris were married in 1938. They had two children – a son, Peter, and a daughter, Susan, and Stan worked as a gardener in the town's park. When he retired, fifteen years ago, he and Doris enjoyed all the time that they now had together, and often went out dancing, which they both loved. Then earlier this year Doris had a stroke and became paralysed on one side of her body. Suddenly, Stan had to do everything for her: washing her, helping her dress, cutting up her food. He could not go out because he was afraid that she would fall, so shopping became a problem. Luckily, the son and daughter both live nearby and can come in to help, but they are both busy and have their own families, so they cannot be there all the time.

Stan wants to look after Doris. He says: 'She would look after me if it was the other way round. I just feel lucky that I still have her.'

The simple fact is, however, that it is becoming harder and harder for Stan to do everything ...

After reading   **1**   Find expressions in the text which mean the opposite of the underlined ones in these sentences.

Example: Stan and Doris <u>disliked</u> the time they had together when he retired.
Stan and Doris *enjoyed* the time they had together.

a   After her stroke, Stan <u>slowly</u> had to do everything for her.
b   He had to help her <u>take off her clothes</u>.
c   <u>Unfortunately</u>, the son and daughter both live <u>a long way away</u>.
d   The son and daughter both <u>have lots of free time</u>.
e   It is becoming <u>easier and easier</u> for Stan to look after Doris.

Revision spot

'Would' and 'Could' (Conditional) sentences

Remember: If + simple past, would/could …

If Stan **was** ill, Doris **would look after** him.
If Stan and Doris **lived** with their son, he **could look after** them.

Practice   Stan and Doris have a difficult decision to make. Doris could stay at home, but that could be difficult for Stan. They could perhaps live with their son or daughter. Or Doris could go into a home. Each idea has its advantages and disadvantages. Make sentences with the words below. Then decide what you think Mr and Mrs Leonard should do.

Example: *If Doris stayed at home, Stan could look after her in her own home.*
If Doris went into a home, …

Doris/stay/at home	Stan/look after/her/in her own home.
	she/get/full-time care/from nurses and doctors.
	be/difficult/for the son or daughter/with their mother and father in their house.
Doris/go/into a home	Mr and Mrs Leonard/perhaps/get/some help like a community nurse/who visit them at home.
	Mr Leonard/have to/do everything for his wife and that/be/very tiring and difficult for him.
Stan and Doris/ live/with their son or daughter	Mr Leonard/visit/his wife there/as often as he wanted to.
	they/have/a comfortable room/and/the son or daughter/look after them.
	Stan and Doris/not be/together/and she/not be/in her own home.

Unit 3 Getting old

Caring for older people

Here is one care worker who works with older people and his job.

While reading **1** This care worker is a 'Care Assistant'. Read the text and find out what kind of work a Care Assistant does. What would you call this job in German?

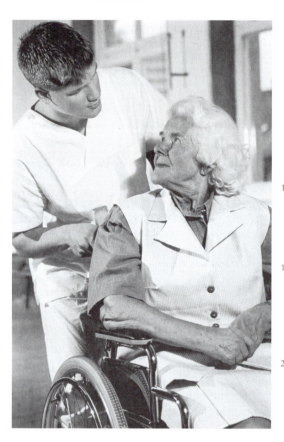

Chris Collins is a 'Care Assistant' in a nursing home. The home has twenty elderly patients who all need 24-hour nursing care. Chris is part of a
5 team which helps the professionally qualified nurses.

"Most of our residents are in their eighties and nineties, and we have one lady who is 103. I begin work at
10 8.00 am, get the patients out of bed, help them wash and dress, and generally make them comfortable. They often ask me to do their hair and make-up. Even when you're elderly
15 it's important to feel and look good!

One of the most important aspects of my job is to make sure the patients are clean and looked after hygienically. So I bathe them, care
20 for small wounds, and treat bedsores if they have them. Some jobs, like taking people to the toilet, are very intimate and it's important to be sensitive.

25 Occasionally, older people get bad-tempered, but it's often because they can't do the things they once did and it's frustrating for them. Some patients want a lot of your time, but you have to understand and be kind.

The nursing home is a pleasant place to work. Patients spend most of the day in the lounge. Relatives can visit when they want, and there are
30 regular visits from the dentist, hairdresser, chiropodist and library visitor.

One of the satisfying parts of this job is that I get to know the patients as individuals and become very fond of them. So it is always sad when someone dies, but the people here are old and you have to expect it. It's good to think that near the end of their days, you have made a difference
35 to their lives and made the quality of them better."

Getting old — **Unit 3**

After reading

2 Complete these sentences to make a short summary of the text.

Where Chris works
a The nursing home where Chris works has ✳✳✳
b It is a very pleasant ✳✳✳
c There is a ✳✳✳ where the patients spend most of the day, and there are visits from professionals like ✳✳✳

The patients
d The residents in the home are mostly ✳✳✳
e Their relatives can ✳✳✳
f They are all old people so you have to expect that ✳✳✳

Chris's work
g Chris helps the professionally ✳✳✳
h He does jobs like ✳✳✳
i He likes the work because ✳✳✳
j One sad thing about the work is ✳✳✳ but ✳✳✳

Important things to remember when you work with older people
k Things like hair and make-up are important for older people because ✳✳✳
l You have to be very sensitive when you do some jobs like ✳✳✳ because ✳✳✳
m You have to remember that older people sometimes get bad tempered because ✳✳✳
n Some patients often want the Care Assistant or nurse all the time which can be difficult, but ✳✳✳

Talking and doing

3 Would you like to do Chris's work? Why? Why not?

4 Look at the picture of Chris and the old lady on the opposite page. What do you think each of them is thinking at the moment?

5 Write a sentence about each of these cartoons.

Vocabulary

Zeichenerklärung: ⚠ Achtung ◄► Gegenteil ≈ (ungefähr) gleichbedeutend mit

to get old	[get 'əʊld]	*alt werden* ⚠ *unregelmäßig*
facts and figures	[ˌfækts ənd 'fɪgəkz]	*Fakten und Zahlen*
image	['ɪmɪdʒ]	*Image*
bad-tempered	[ˌbæd'tempəd]	*schlecht gelaunt*
forgetful	[fə'getfl]	*vergesslich*
to expect	[ɪk'spekt]	*erwarten*
total	['təʊtl]	*Gesamt-*
therefore	['ðeəfɔː]	*deshalb*
politician	[ˌpɒlə'tɪʃn]	*Politiker/in*
growing number (of)	[ˌgrəʊɪŋ 'nʌmbər əv]	*eine wachsende Zahl (von)*
society	[sə'saɪəti]	*Gesellschaft*
medicine	['medsɪn]	*Medikament*
pension	['penʃn]	*Rente* ⚠ *Aussprache*
to support	[sə'pɔːt]	*(finanziell) unterstützen*
statistics	[stə'tɪstɪks]	*Statistiken*
third age	[ˌθɜːd 'eɪdʒ]	*dritter Lebensabschnitt*
retirement	[rɪ'taɪəmənt]	*Pensionierung*
retired	[rɪ'taɪəd]	*pensioniert*
pedal power	['pedl paʊə]	*Pedalen Power*
advertisement	[əd'vɜːtɪsmənt]	*Anzeige* ≈ **ad, advert**
history	['hɪstri]	*Geschichte*
headmaster	[ˌhed'mɑːstə]	*Schulleiter*
a bit of a fitness fan	['fɪtnəs fæn]	*ein ziemlicher Fitness Fan*
a couple of years ago	[ə ˌkʌpl əv jɪəz ə'gəʊ]	*vor ein paar Jahren*
for charity	[fə 'tʃærəti]	*zu wohltätigen Zwecken*
to raise	[reɪz]	*sammeln*
Children in Need	[ˌtʃɪldrən ɪn 'niːd]	*Kinder in Not (Wohlfahrtsgesellschaft)*
if you feel like joining us	[ɪf ju ˌfiːl laɪk 'dʒɔɪnɪŋ ʌs]	*wenn dir danach ist, mitzufahren*
Roman	['rəʊmən]	*römisch*
guide	[gaɪd]	*Reiseleiter/in*
accommodation	[əˌkɒmə'deɪʃn]	*Unterkunft*
to arrange	[ə'reɪndʒ]	*arrangieren*
Highlands	['haɪləndz]	*(das schottische) Hochland*
touring holiday	[ˌtʊərɪŋ 'hɒlədeɪ]	*Rundreise*
banquet	['bæŋkwɪt]	*Bankett*
freepost	['friːpəʊst]	*Porto zahlt Empfänger*
olive	['ɒlɪv]	*Olive*
wild flower	[waɪld 'flaʊə]	*Wildblume*
villa	['vɪlə]	*Villa*
non-painting partners	[ˌnɒn 'peɪntɪŋ pɑːtnəz]	*nicht-malende Partner*
language course	['læŋgwɪdʒ kɔːs]	*Sprachkurs*
level	['levl]	*Niveau*
carefully	['keəfəli]	*sorgfältig*

Vocabulary — Unit 3

decision	[dɪˈsɪʒn]	*Entscheidung*
neighbour	[ˈneɪbə]	*Nachbar/in*
carer	[ˈkeərə]	*Pfleger/in*
wedding day	[ˈwedɪŋ deɪ]	*Hochzeitstag*
to have a stroke	[həv ə ˈstrəʊk]	*einen Schlaganfall erleiden*
		⚠ *unregelmäßig*
paralysed	[ˈpærəlaɪzd]	*gelähmt*
nearby	[ˈnɪəbaɪ]	*nahe gelegen, in der Nähe*
the simple fact is that	[ðə ˌsɪmpl ˈfækt ɪz ðət]	*Tatsache ist …*
to dislike	[dɪsˈlaɪk]	*nicht mögen* ◄► **to like**
slowly	[ˈsləʊli]	*langsam* ◄► **quickly**
conditional sentence	[kənˌdɪʃənl ˈsentəns]	*Konditionalsatz*
comfortable	[ˈkʌmftəbl]	*bequem*
nursing home	[ˈnɜːsɪŋ həʊm]	*Pflegeheim*
elderly	[ˈeldəli]	*älter*
patient	[ˈpeɪʃnt]	*Patient/in*
nursing care	[ˈnɜːsɪŋ keə]	*Pflege*
professionally qualified	[prəˌfeʃənəli ˈkwɒlɪfaɪd]	*qualifiziert*
resident	[ˈrezɪdənt]	*Bewohner/in*
in their eighties/ nineties	[ɪn ðeər ˈeɪtiz/ˈnaɪntiz]	*mit 80/90 Jahren*
aspect	[ˈæspekt]	*Aspekt*
hygienically	[haɪˈdʒiːnɪkli]	*hygienisch*
to bathe	[beɪð]	*baden*
wound	[wuːnd]	*Wunde*
to treat	[triːt]	*behandeln*
bedsore	[ˈbedsɔː]	*wundgelegene Stelle*
to take someone to the toilet	[teɪk tə ðə ˈtɔɪlət]	*jdn zur Toilette bringen*
		⚠ *unregelmäßig*
intimate	[ˈɪntɪmət]	*intim*
sensitive	[ˈsensətɪv]	*sensibel*
		⚠ **sensible** – *vernünftig*
occasionally	[əˈkeɪʒənəli]	*gelegentlich*
frustrating	[frʌˈstreɪtɪŋ]	*frustrierend*
pleasant	[ˈpleznt]	*angenehm*
lounge	[laʊndʒ]	*Gesellschaftsraum*
regular	[ˈregjələ]	*regelmäßig* ◄► **irregular**
dentist	[ˈdentɪst]	*Zahnarzt, Zahnärztin*
hairdresser	[ˈheədresə]	*Friseur/Friseuse*
chiropodist	[kɪˈrɒpədɪst]	*Fußpfleger/in*
individual (n)	[ˌɪndɪˈvɪdʒuəl]	*Einzelne/r*
to become fond (of)	[bɪˈkʌm fɒnd əv]	*beginnen, jdn zu mögen*
		⚠ *unregelmäßig*
		I became very fond of her.
to make a difference (to)	[meɪk ə ˈdɪfrəns]	*einen Unterschied bei etwas machen hier: einen entscheidenden Beitrag leisten* ⚠ *unregelmäßig*
summary	[ˈsʌməri]	*Zusammenfassung*
at the moment	[ət ðə ˈməʊmənt]	*im Augenblick*

4 Everyone is a person

> Inside everyone there is a person. It is something that we can easily forget – especially if what we see on the outside is someone who is disabled, or finding life extremely difficult and needs our help. The young girl in this story was very lucky: she had good friends and a great family who understood.

Damita's accident

While reading 1 This true story is from a young people's magazine. Find a good title for it. (You can see the title that the magazine used on page 35. Is yours better?)

Damita with her Mum, Dad and Jonathan Coombes, who saved her life.

'I was 16 when I had my accident. I was going into town to meet some friends and had just started to cross the road at a pedestrian crossing when a car suddenly appeared and hit me. It was a man in a garden nearby who saved my life. His name was Jonathan and he was a nurse.

I was in a coma for four months after that. When I opened my eyes, mum and dad were there. They explained I had been in an accident, and it had damaged my brain so that I could not move or talk. I really felt like a baby again! I could not remember things, either – some days I forgot if I had eaten, and dad even had to push up the corners of my mouth to show me how to smile!

During the next few months, I had to learn to walk, read, write and talk again. My mum and dad were always there and they were great. They did not spoil me and always told me the truth about what was happening. And my friends were fantastic. They came to see me every day in hospital. One friend Vicky used to take me to the school dances on Saturdays. I had always loved dancing, but doing it in a wheelchair was a bit different!

It was not until about a year after the accident that I went back to school to do my 'A' levels. I still used a stick to walk, but one day my friend Jenny took it away, saying I did not need it. I have been walking without it ever since.

I still forget things, but I have a cassette recorder in lessons that I can listen to at home. I have started ballet and swimming again, too.

As for the future, I want to be a primary school teacher. I always planned to study at university, and I am not going to let my accident stop me!'

Damita re-learning the basics after her accident

After reading

2 Answer these questions about the text.

a Who saved Damita's life?
b Who took her to school dances in a wheelchair?
c Who showed her how to smile again?
d How did her parents help her most?
e How did she begin walking again without a stick?
f How does she help herself to remember her lessons?
g What did she love doing before the accident and has just begun doing again?
h What does Damita plan to do in the future?

Talking and doing

3 Work with a partner or in a small group. Write a short text in which you tell Damita's story again from the point of view of either a) her parents or b) one of her schoolfriends. Talk about what happened, how you felt, how you tried to help. Begin like this:

a *One morning we suddenly had a phone call from the hospital. They said our daughter had had an accident …*
b *One morning, our class teacher told us that Damita had had an accident and that she was in hospital in a coma …*

4 From this text, what do you think is the best way to help a person who, like Damita, is disabled? Try to write down three helpful 'rules', using these expressions:

You must/must not/don't (ever) … /(always) try to …

(The title was: '16 – but I had to learn to walk and talk again.')

Unit 4 Everyone is a person

Down's Syndrome

For all disabled people, it is terribly important to be accepted, and to lead a 'normal' life. But as many find, it is not always that easy ...

While reading

1 Write down the most important facts about the story in this newspaper article.

Who?
Where?
What is happening?
Why?
What next?

School says 'no' to Down's Syndrome pupil

A school in Newcastle has refused to accept a girl with Down's Syndrome as a pupil next year.

11 year-old Carla Morrison has been a pupil at the nearby primary school for six years and now wants to go with her friends to the local secondary school. But the school has said 'no' to Carla's parents.

'We do not feel that this is the right place for Carla,' the headteacher said today. 'She needs small classes and special teachers that we do not have.'

11 year-old Carla Morrison

Carla's parents, who are both teachers themselves, are angry about the school's decision. 'It is quite ridiculous,' Carla's mother said. 'Carla loves school and being with her friends. She has managed perfectly well for the last six years. If she needs extra help, we can give it to her.'

Mr and Mrs Morrison plan to appeal against the school's decision. Mr Morrison said, 'We will take the case to the European Court if necessary. This is not just about our daughter: it affects all children with Down's Syndrome everywhere.'

Talking and doing

2 Who do you think is right? The school or Carla's parents? Give your reasons.

3 Do you think it is easy for disabled people in our society to lead a 'normal' life? Talk about one of these things in a group, then tell the class your ideas.

   a   Towns and buildings. Are they easy for disabled people to use?
   b   Jobs. Do disabled people have the same possibilities as people who are not disabled?
   c   Entertainment and free time. Is there as much for disabled people to do as people who are not disabled?
   d   Public transport. Are buses and trains easy for disabled people to use?
   e   Your school. What problems do/could disabled students at your school have?

Revision spot

Sentences with 'who' and 'which' (relative sentences)

Carla's parents, **who** are both teachers, are angry about the decision.

The school, **which** is just outside Newcastle, refused to accept Carla.

When you are writing, you can often put extra information into a sentence with 'who' (for people) and 'which' (for things). You must put commas before and after this extra information!

Practice

Write these sentences again as one sentence. Use *who* and *which*.

Example: Carla has Down's Syndrome. She wants to go to the local secondary school.
Carla, who has Down's Syndrome, wants to …

   a   The school has said 'no'. It is in Newcastle.
   b   Mr Jones says the school is not the right place for Carla. He is the headteacher.
   c   He thinks that the classes in the school are too big for Carla. The classes can have thirty or more pupils in them.
   d   Carla's parents are very angry. They think the decision is ridiculous.
   e   They think Carla will be fine at secondary school. She loved primary school and managed perfectly well there.
   f   Mr Morrison plans to appeal against the decision to the European Court. He thinks the decision affects all children with Down's Syndrome.

Unit 4   Everyone is a person

Caring for the homeless

A home is one of our most basic needs: without one,
it is very difficult to keep our dignity.
But every large city has its homeless people – many under 25.
This song by Phil Collins describes their life.

Another Day In Paradise

She calls out to the man in the street
'Sir, can you help me?
It's cold and I've nowhere to sleep,
Is there somewhere you can tell me?'

He walks on, doesn't look back
He pretends he can't hear her.
Starts to whistle as he crosses the street
Seems embarrassed to be there.

    Oh think twice, 'cos it's another day for
    You and me in paradise
    Oh, think twice
    It's just another day for
    You, you and me in paradise.

She calls out to the man in the street
He can see she's been crying.
She's got blisters on the soles of her feet
She can't walk but she's trying.

    Oh, think twice ...
    Oh Lord, is there nothing more anybody can do
    Oh Lord, there must be something you can say

You can tell from the lines on her face
You can see that she's been there
Probably been moved on from every place
'Cos she didn't fit in there.

    Oh, think twice ...

Everyone is a person　　Unit 4

After reading

1 Answer these questions and tell the story of the song in your own words.

　a Who (do you think) the 'she' in the song could be?
　b What do we learn about her?
　c What do you think the line in the song 'You can see that she's been there' means?
　d Who (do you think) 'the man in the street' is? Describe him a little.
　e What happens in the song?
　f Why (do you think) the man in the street does what he does?
　g What (do you think) 'she' and 'the man in the street' both do next? What are they both thinking now?

Talking and doing

2 The song seems very simple. But, like all good songs, it is complicated when you think more about it. Work in a group. Talk about the questions below, then tell the class your ideas.

　a The song is called 'Another Day In Paradise'. Can you explain the title?
　b What do you think Phil Collins wants to say with these lines?

　　Oh Lord, is there nothing more anybody can do
　　Oh Lord, there must be something you can say

　c Which of these do you think best explains the meaning of the song?

　　• *Homeless people have a terrible life.*
　　• *We all know that there are homeless people, but we prefer to think that they do not exist.*
　　• *We all want to help homeless people, but we do not know how.*

3 People often say (or think) that homeless people are only homeless because they are lazy, or even because they choose to be. 'Everyone can get a home or a job if they need one and really want it!' What do you think?

4 Look at the photograph of the two-year old girl. Talk about her and her mother's situation.

Unit 4 Everyone is a person

The Samaritans

There are times in everyone's life when they need someone to talk to. An organization (in Britain) which listens is the Samaritans.

While reading **1** Find the headlines below which go with each paragraph of the text.

A Part of a family
B Learning to be a Samaritan
C Who are the Samaritans?
D Who calls the Samaritans?
E Samaritans don't tell you what to do

Rachel works for three hours each week and all night once a month. Like all Samaritans she tells very few people that she does it: it could be very difficult if a neighbour called with a problem and knew she was speaking to Rachel.

The Samaritans have existed in Britain for more than 40 years. It is an organization which listens to those who need someone to talk to. All its workers are unpaid volunteers, ordinary people who want to help.

The Samaritans have offices where people can come, but almost all
5 telephone. The people who call are of all types and all ages: doctors, bank managers, schoolchildren, housewives, the elderly. They may be lonely, ill, have problems with their marriage, or have just lost someone near to them. There is no typical caller.

People who become a Samaritan need a period of training. This lasts six
weeks. They have to know and think about difficult ideas like suicide,
AIDS, child abuse and death. They must learn to be good listeners, and
never to judge people.

Samaritans listen, they do not tell people what they must do; they
never say 'I know how you feel' (as Rachel says, 'I probably don't know
how they feel at all'); and they will never tell another person about a
conversation which they have had: not the police, not a school, not even
a parent.

Listening to people's problems can be very difficult and it is important
that Samaritans themselves have people they can talk to. There are
always other volunteers around so that, as Rachel says, 'At the end of a
long night you don't need to take all the problems home with you.
Being a Samaritan is like being part of a large family. We all help each
other'.

After reading

2 True or false? If false, give a true statement.

a Samaritans are paid for their work.
b Most of the people who want help come to a Samaritan office.
c It takes almost a year to become a Samaritan.
d The Samaritans will tell you what you must do to make your situation better.
e Samaritans often need to talk to other Samaritans after they have had a very difficult phone call.

3 Explain in your own words.

a (The people who call) … have just lost someone near to them. (line 5)
b There is no typical caller. (line 8)
c They must learn … never to judge people. (lines 11–12)
d You don't need to take all the problems home with you. (line 21)

Talking and doing

4 The Samaritans have a number of important rules. Talk about them in a small group.

a Samaritans listen, they do not give advice. What do you think about this?
b A child runs away from home and comes to a Samaritan office. The Samaritans will tell no one. What do you feel about this?
c People, especially young people, sometimes call the Samaritans 'as a joke'. The Samaritan who answers always talks to them and never tells them they are 'stupid'. Why do you think he or she does this?

5 Samaritans are 'ordinary people' – not experts like priests, doctors or psychologists. What do you feel about this?

Vocabulary

Zeichenerklärung: ⚠ Achtung ◆▶ Gegenteil ≈ (ungefähr) gleichbedeutend mit

especially	[ɪˈspeʃəli]	*besonders*
		I ~ liked her last film.
pedestrian crossing	[pəˌdestrɪən ˈkrɒsɪŋ]	*Fußgängerüberweg*
to save someone's life	[seɪv sʌmwʌnz ˈlaɪf]	*jdm das Leben retten*
coma	[ˈkəʊmə]	*Koma*
to damage	[ˈdæmɪdʒ]	*schaden*
brain	[breɪn]	*Gehirn*
to push the corners of one's mouth up	[pʊʃ ðə ˈkɔːnəz əv wʌnz maʊθ ʌp]	*die Mundwinkel nach oben ziehen*
to spoil	[spɔɪl]	*verwöhnen*
		vgl. Adjektiv: **spoilt** – *verwöhnt*
		a spoilt child
truth	[truːθ]	*Wahrheit*
		vgl. Adjektiv: **true** – *wahr*
		to tell the truth – *die Wahrheit sagen*
fantastic	[fænˈtæstɪk]	*fantastisch*
		≈ **brilliant, wonderful**
wheelchair	[ˈwiːltʃeə]	*Rollstuhl*
a bit	[ə ˈbɪt]	*ein bißchen*
A-levels	[ˈeɪ levlz]	*(entspricht) Abitur*
stick	[stɪk]	*Gehstock*
		≈ **walking stick**
cassette recorder	[kəˈset rɪkɔːdə]	*Kassettenrekorder*
ballet	[ˈbæleɪ]	*Ballett*
primary school teacher	[ˈpraɪməri skuːl tiːtʃə]	*Grundschullehrer/in*
university	[juːnɪˈvɜːsəti]	*Universität*
point of view	[ˌpɔɪnt əv ˈvjuː]	*Standpunkt*
		What's your ~ on …?
helpful	[ˈhelpfl]	*nützlich*
		sonst auch: *hilfsbereit*
rule	[ruːl]	*Regel*
Down's syndrome	[ˈdaʊnz sɪndrəʊm]	*Down Syndrom*
to accept	[əkˈsept]	*anerkennen*
to lead (one's life)	[liːd wʌnz ˈlaɪf]	*sein Leben führen*
		⚠ *unregelmäßig*
pupil	[ˈpjuːpl]	*Schüler/in*
local secondary school	[ˌləʊkl ˈsekəndri skuːl]	*örtliche Schule (Sekundarstufe I)*
special	[ˈspeʃl]	*Spezial-*
ridiculous	[rɪˈdɪkjələs]	*lächerlich*
		Don't be so ~.
to manage	[ˈmænɪdʒ]	*schaffen*
		sonst auch: *leiten*
perfectly well	[ˈpɜːfɪktli wel]	*tadellos*

to appeal (against)	[əˈpiːl əgenst]	*Einspruch erheben gegen*
to affect	[əˈfekt]	*betreffen*
possibility(-ies)	[ˌpɒsəˈbɪləti]	*Möglichkeit*
		vgl. Adjektiv: **possible** – *möglich*
relative sentence	[ˈrelətɪv sentəns]	*Relativsatz*
comma	[ˈkɒmə]	*Komma*
homeless	[ˈhəʊmləs]	*obdachlos*
		~ **people live on the streets.**
basic need	[ˌbeɪsɪk ˈniːd]	*Grundbedürfnis*
dignity	[ˈdɪgnəti]	*Würde*
paradise	[ˈpærədaɪs]	*Paradies*
		◄► **hell** – *Hölle*
to call out (to someone)	[ˌkɔːl ˈaʊt tə]	*jdn ansprechen*
to pretend	[prɪˈtend]	*so tun, als ob*
to whistle	[ˈwɪsl]	*pfeifen*
embarrassed	[ɪmˈbærəst]	*verlegen*
		vgl. Adjektiv: **embarrassing** – *peinlich*
'cos (= because)	[kɒz]	*weil*
to cry	[kraɪ]	*weinen*
blister	[ˈblɪstə]	*Blase*
sole of one's foot	[səʊl]	*(Fuß-)Sohle*
Lord	[lɔːd]	*Herr*
to fit in	[ˌfɪt ˈɪn]	*dazu gehören*
line	[laɪn]	*Falte*
to move (someone) on	[ˌmuːv ˈɒn]	*vertreiben*
simple	[ˈsɪmpl]	*einfach*
complicated	[ˈkɒmplɪkeɪtɪd]	*kompliziert*
to exist	[ɪgˈzɪst]	*existieren*
(the good) Samaritan	[ðə ˌgʊd səˈmærɪtən]	*der barmherzige Samariter*
unpaid	[ˌʌnˈpeɪd]	*unbezahlt*
		vgl. Verb: **to pay** – *bezahlen*
to call (= to telephone)	[kɔːl]	*anrufen*
		I'll call him tomorrow.
the elderly	[ði ˈeldəli]	*die Älteren*
marriage	[ˈmærɪdʒ]	*Ehe*
period of training	[ˌpɪəriəd əv ˈtreɪnɪŋ]	*Trainingsphase*
suicide	[ˈsuːɪsaɪd]	*Selbstmord*
		to commit ~
death	[deθ]	*Tod*
		vgl. Adjektiv: **dead** – *tot*
listener	[ˈlɪsnə]	*Zuhörer/in*
		She's a good ~.
to judge	[dʒʌdʒ]	*verurteilen*
		vgl. Nomen: **judge** – *Richter/in*
as a joke	[əz ə ˈdʒəʊk]	*zum Spaß*
priest	[priːst]	*Priester/in*
psychologist	[saɪˈkɒlədʒɪst]	*Psychologe, Psychologin*

5 A home of your own

My place

People live in different ways at different times in their lives – so they need different types of homes.

While reading 1 Copy and fill in the table about these people. You will need to 'read between the lines' for some of the answers.

	age	money	children	description of home (rooms, furniture …)
Brenda and Larry	×××	×××	×××	×××
Mark and Penny	×××	×××	×××	×××
Sally	×××	×××	×××	×××

Brenda and Larry are in their late forties, and have three grown-up children. Their home is a bit unusual – it is an old primary school which they bought two years ago and are turning into a 'normal' house. Brenda: 'The house is a lot of work but we really enjoy it. We've done
5 most of the work ourselves. When the children were small, we lived in the town. They always wanted to go somewhere, so it was better. But now they're grown up, we like living in this village. Our oldest son has already left home, and I suppose that the other two will leave soon. The house will seem very empty without them!'

10 Mark and Penny are in their mid-twenties. They both have jobs and are planning to get married next year. They have just rented their first small flat together.

15 Mark: 'Help! A few years ago all I thought about was going out with my mates. Now I'm going to get married, have got a flat, and spend my weekends looking at sofas! But
20 it's great and Penny and I are really excited about it. The only problem is my mum and dad – they want to do everything for us. It's hard to be tactful, sometimes!'

25 Sally has just left college and has got her first job. She lives in a flat with four other people: they all have their own rooms but share the kitchen, bathroom and living room.

Sally: 'I love
30 having my own room. I haven't got much furniture and I
35 suppose you might think that what's in the room is 'junk'. I cer-
40 tainly got all of it cheap! But it's what I

like – posters, some old model cars, an Indian rug ... The most expensive thing I own is my collection of CDs. The best thing about having a
45 room? It's mine – I can do what I want with it. The biggest problem? I'm very tidy but some of my flatmates aren't. It drives me crazy!'

After reading 2 Now say in two or three sentences why 'people need different types of homes at different times in their lives' and what those types are.

Talking and doing 3 Work in a group of three to five people. You are all going to share a flat – like Sally's. But will you get on well together?

a First make a short list of your 'good' and 'bad' habits (Are you tidy? Are you bad-tempered in the morning? ...).
b Now make some rules for living together.
c Is there one of you who should definitely find another flat?

Unit 5 A home of your own

Who does what at home?

Before reading **1** What are the jobs that have to be done in a home? Do you think some are for men and some for women? Is 'who does what' changing, do you think?

Who does what at home?

	What happens			What people think should happen		
	Mainly man	Mainly woman	Shared equally	Mainly man	Mainly woman	Shared equally
Household shopping	8	45	47	1	22	76
Makes evening meal	9	70	20	1	39	58
Washes up	28	33	37	12	11	76
Does household cleaning	4	68	27	1	36	62
Does washing and ironing	3	84	12	–	58	40
Household repairs (DIY)	82	6	10	66	1	31
Organizes household money	31	40	28	17	14	66
Looks after sick children	1	60	39	–	37	60
Teaches children discipline	9	17	73	8	4	85

Philip's diary

So what is it like being 'mum'? This teenage boy, Philip, decided to find out. He did all the housework in his family for a week. This is his diary.

Monday
The first jobs tonight were the ironing and washing. They took ages! I'd never used the washing machine before so mum had to show me which programme
5 I needed. Next time I'll know.

Tuesday
Made breakfast and cleaned the living room. The glass door was covered in fingerprints so I put up a notice saying: 'Don't touch this glass again if you want to
10 live'. After school, made spaghetti bolognese for dinner.

Wednesday
I can't believe how much washing there is, especially from my little brother, Michael. There was a fingerprint on the glass door and I got really angry until I realised it was mine. After school, went to the
15 supermarket. I couldn't find the money that mum had given me and I didn't quite have enough to pay. A woman behind me gave me 71p. Did some more ironing and made dinner out of a packet. Not too bad.

Thursday
Was late for school! Made beans on toast for dinner. Mum and dad were in the living room watching Top Of The Pops on television. Talk about changing roles!

Friday
I have a routine now and things are getting easier. After breakfast I loaded the dishwasher and checked the living room. Cooked burgers for dinner with lots of extra onions. Dad said he didn't like onions on burgers!

Saturday
Too tired to do anything. The living room was a mess and the door was covered in fingerprints. Dad bought us a takeaway for dinner.

Sunday
Great! Everyone was out so I got up late, cleaned the living room and was having a rest when dad phoned and asked if I'd done the shopping. I said I'd do it later. He said the supermarket would be closed soon. Bought some pizza, but they all got back late and the food was cold. Why can't people be more thoughtful? Don't they realise how hard it all is??!!

After reading

2 Look at the 'Who does what at home' table.

a Which jobs do women do mainly, and which do men do?
b Which job seems to be almost completely a 'woman's job'?
c Which job is almost completely a 'man's job'?
d Which job is shared most equally?
e How – generally – would work in the home change if we all did what people think should happen?

3 Work with a partner and write down your answers to these questions then compare them to those of another pair of students.

a Make a list of the jobs that Philip did all week. What problems did he have with each one?
b What do you think was his worst day? Why?
c What do you think was his best day?
d What do you think he learned from the week?
e Philip had to go to school all week as well as do the housework. So do you think this was a fair test for him?

Talking and doing

4 Talk about these questions in a group, then tell the class your ideas.

a Why are the jobs that men and women do in the home changing?
b Do you think they are changing quickly enough? Why? Why not?

Unit 5　A home of your own

Safety in the home

Homes can be dangerous places.
More people are hurt in accidents in the home than at work,
and almost as many as in accidents on the road.

Talking and doing

1　This bathroom is a catastrophe. Look at the picture, and make sentences about the dangers in it. Use the table on the next page.

You could/ might	cut yourself with get an electric shock from get scalded by get poisoned by set fire to something (with) burn yourself (with) fall out of drown (in) be suffocated (by)	the matches * the soap * the mat * the cigarettes * the medicine * the pills * the electric fire * the disin- fectant * the radio * the hair-dryer * the hot water * the gas * the bleach * the window * the scissors * the razorblade * the bathtub

2 Now think of another room or place in the home (the kitchen, garage …) and make two more sentences about it and its dangers.

Revision spot

Talking about the future

When you are sure (or fairly sure) about something in the future you can say:

It **will definitely rain** tomorrow.
Germany **will (almost) certainly win** the football match!

When you are only about 50 per cent sure, you can use 'may':

It **may rain**, but I'm not sure. (It may not!)

When you are not sure at all (only about 10–20 per cent), or if you really think that it won't happen at all, use 'might' or 'could':

Well, they **could win**, but they are not playing very well at the moment!

Practice

Complete this text about homes in the future with a partner. Use *will* (*definitely/almost certainly*), *may* or *might/could* to show how sure you are about each thing.

Homes in the future (1) *will almost certainly be* (to be) very different from those which we live in now. People (2) *** (to need) many of the rooms that we have now – a bedroom, a kitchen, a living room – but with more and more free-time they (3) *** (to want) another room for their hobbies, too, rather like what the Americans call a 'den'. Also, working from home (4) *** (to become) more popular in the future and that (5) *** (to mean) another room as an office. We (6) *** (to see) changes in the kitchen, with more electrical equipment. But it is in the living room that there (7) *** (to be) the biggest changes, as the television/computer becomes the way in which we not only watch TV, but shop, send letters and look after our money. And in 50 years' time every house (8) *** (to own) its own robot!

Unit 5 A home of your own

A dream kitchen

Before reading   **1**   Here is a typical modern fitted kitchen. How many things in it can you name?

Designing a kitchen

Your kitchen is the one of the most important rooms in your home and really needs to be designed well. Here are a few tips.

It is often more than just the place where you cook. You may eat there, or wash clothes and iron; it may be your 'hobbies room' or the place
5   where children play or do homework. Think about the different ways you want to use your kitchen when you design it.

A home of your own   Unit 5

When you are cooking, the cooker, fridge, cupboards and work surfaces must be close together – the so-called 'work triangle'.

If you do not want to spending hours when you are cooking just walking from place to place, remember the work triangle – cooker, work-surfaces, fridge and cupboards: they must all be close together. If you
10   have a dishwasher, make sure it is near the cupboards where you keep the cups and plates.

Choose tiles or wallpaper for the walls that are easy to clean. Lights are important and you need plenty of them. If you have a window, think if you want it near the sink: curtains near a cooker can be dangerous.

Talking and doing

2   Design a kitchen! Here is a plan of the kitchen in your new flat. At the moment it has nothing – just a door and two windows. Work in a group and draw a design for the kitchen showing where you want to put everything. Use the tips you have just read.

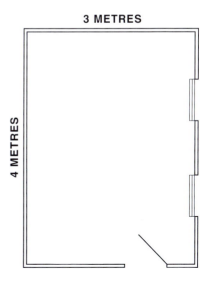

Useful phrases for making suggestions

Why don't we …?
We could …
What if we (put) …?
How about (putting) …?
Let's …

51

Unit 5 A home of your own

Vocabulary

Zeichenerklärung: ⚠ Achtung ◀▶ Gegenteil ≈ (ungefähr) gleichbedeutend mit

description	[dɪˈskrɪpʃn]	*Beschreibung*
in their late forties	[ɪn ðeə leɪt ˈfɔːtiz]	*in den späten Vierzigern*
grown-up	[ˈɡrəʊnʌp]	*erwachsen*
primary school	[ˈpraɪməri skuːl]	*Grundschule*
to turn (something into something)	[ˌtɜːn ˈɪntə]	*umbauen*
in their mid-twenties	[ɪn ðeə mɪdˈtwentiz]	*in den Mittzwanzigern*
to rent	[rent]	*mieten* auch Nomen: *Miete*
mate	[meɪt]	*Kumpel*
excited	[ɪkˈsaɪtɪd]	*(freudig) aufgeregt*
tactful	[ˈtæktfl]	*taktvoll*
own	[ˈəʊn]	*eigene/r*
to share	[ʃeə]	*sich teilen*
living room	[ˈlɪvɪŋ ruːm]	*Wohnzimmer*
furniture	[ˈfɜːnɪtʃə]	*Möbel*
I suppose	[aɪ səˈpəʊz]	*ich nehme an*
junk (Umgangssprache)	[dʒʌŋk]	*Gerümpel*
Indian rug	[ˈɪndiən rʌɡ]	*indischer Teppich*
collection	[kəˈlekʃn]	*Sammlung*
to drive someone crazy	[draɪv ˈkreɪzi]	*jdn zur Verzweiflung treiben* ⚠ *unregelmäßig*
to get on well together	[ɡet ˈɒn ˈwel teɡeðə]	*gut miteinander auskommen* ⚠ *unregelmäßig*
habit	[ˈhæbɪt]	*Angewohnheit*
definitely	[ˈdefɪnətli]	*auf jeden Fall*
survey	[ˈsɜːveɪ]	*Umfrage*
figure	[ˈfɪɡə]	*Zahl*
shared equally	[ʃeəd ˈiːkwəli]	*zu gleichen Teilen*
to make a meal	[meɪk ə ˈmiːl]	*eine Mahlzeit zubereiten* ⚠ *unregelmäßig*
to wash up	[ˌwɒʃ ˈʌp]	*abwaschen*
to clean	[kliːn]	*putzen*
to iron	[ˈaɪən]	*bügeln*
repairs	[rɪˈpeə]	*Reparaturen*
DIY (= Do It Yourself)	[ˌdiː aɪ ˈwaɪ]	*Heimwerken*
sick	[sɪk]	*krank*
discipline	[ˈdɪsəplɪn]	*Disziplin*
diary	[ˈdaɪəri]	*Tagebuch* sonst auch: *Kalender*
it took ages	[ɪt tʊk ˈeɪdʒɪz]	*es dauerte ewig*
covered in	[ˈkʌvəd ɪn]	*bedeckt mit*
fingerprint	[ˈfɪŋɡəprɪnt]	*Fingerabdruck*
notice	[ˈnəʊtɪs]	*Zettel*
to touch	[tʌtʃ]	*anfassen*

Vocabulary — Unit 5

packet	['pækɪt]	*Packung*
beans on toast	[biːnz ɒn 'təʊst]	*gebackene Bohnen auf Toast*
Top of the Pops	[ˌtɒp əv ðə 'pɒps]	*Hitparade (englische Fernsehsendung)*
to change roles	[tʃeɪndʒ 'rəʊlz]	*die Rollen tauschen*
onion	['ʌnjən]	*Zwiebel*
a mess	[mes]	*Unordnung*
takeaway	['teɪkəweɪ]	*Essen zum mitnehmen*
to have a rest	[həv ə 'rest]	*sich ausruhen* ⚠ unregelmäßig
burger	['bɜːgə]	*Hamburger* ⚠ Aussprache
thoughtful	['θɔːtfl]	*rücksichtsvoll*
pair	[peə]	*Paar*
safety	['seɪfti]	*Sicherheit*
to be hurt	[bi 'hɜːt]	*verletzt werden* ⚠ unregelmäßig
catastrophe	[kə'tæstrəfi]	*Katastrophe* ⚠ Aussprache
to get an electric shock	[get ən ɪ'lektrɪk ʃɒk]	*einen Stromschlag bekommen* ⚠ unregelmäßig
to get scalded	[get 'skɔldɪd]	*sich verbrühen* ⚠ unregelmäßig
to get poisoned	[get 'pɔɪznd]	*sich vergiften* ⚠ unregelmäßig
to set fire (to)	[set 'faɪə tə]	*in Brand stecken* ⚠ unregelmäßig
to burn oneself	[bɜːn wʌnself]	*sich verbrennen*
to drown	[draʊn]	*ertrinken*
to be suffocated	[bi 'sʌfəkeɪtɪd]	*erstickt werden* ⚠ unregelmäßig
match	[mætʃ]	*Streichholz*
soap	[səʊp]	*Seife*
mat	[mæt]	*Matte*
pill	[pɪl]	*Pille*
disinfectant	[ˌdɪsɪn'fektənt]	*Desinfektionsmittel*
hair dryer	['heədraɪə]	*Fön*
gas	[gæs]	*Gas*
bleach	[bliːtʃ]	*Bleichmittel*
razor(blade)	['reɪzəbleɪd]	*Rasierklinge*
bathtub	['bɑːθtʌb]	*Badewanne*
den	[den]	*Hobbyraum*
dream kitchen	['driːm kɪtʃɪn]	*Traumküche*
fitted kitchen	[ˌfɪtɪd 'kɪtʃɪn]	*Einbauküche*
to design	[dɪ'zaɪn]	*entwerfen*
tip	[tɪp]	*Hinweis*
cooker	['kʊkə]	*Herd*
fridge	[frɪdʒ]	*Kühlschrank* Abkürzung von **refrigerator**
worksurface	['wɜːksɜːfɪs]	*Arbeitsfläche*
close together	[kləʊs tə'geðə]	*nahe beisammen*
work-triangle	['wɜːktraɪæŋgl]	*Arbeitsecke*
dishwasher	['dɪʃwɒʃə]	*Geschirrspülmaschine*
tile	[taɪl]	*Fliese*
wallpaper	['wɔːlpeɪpə]	*Tapete*
sink	[sɪŋk]	*Spülbecken*
curtain	['kɜːtn]	*Vorhang*
to draw	[drɔː]	*zeichnen* ⚠ unregelmäßig
suggestion	[sə'dʒestʃən]	*Vorschlag*

6 Staying healthy

As a homemaker or a care worker, you will need to know all about staying healthy – for yourself, and for the people that you care for. One aspect of good health is a healthy diet.

A healthy diet

While reading 1 You probably know the most important facts already about a healthy diet. Read this page and decide where these missing words belong.

*pasta * nice * low * carrots * high * cheese * chicken * different*

Healthy food

Healthy food is low in sugar, low in fat, (1) ✳✳✳ in salt and (2) ✳✳✳ in natural fibre (not highly 'processed').

A balanced diet

For a healthy diet, we need foods every day which together give us all the (3) ✳✳✳ things which we need. People often talk about the Four Food Groups. A 'balanced' diet would have some foods from each group every day.

The four food groups

Food group	Examples
starchy food ('carbohydrates')	bread, (4) ✳✳✳, rice, cereals, potatoes
dairy products	milk, (5) ✳✳✳, yogurt, eggs
meat and meat alternatives	pork, lamb, beef, (6) ✳✳✳, fish, cheese, eggs, beans, lentils, nuts
vegetables and fruit	(7) ✳✳✳, courgettes, cabbage, salads, tomatoes, bananas, oranges, apples, pears

Enjoy your food!

Finally, and perhaps most important, you should enjoy what you eat! No one will eat a healthy diet if the food tastes horrible. It can be healthy and (8) ✳✳✳!

After reading

2 Explain why these foods are not so healthy.

    a burgers and chips
    b cake and biscuits
    c peanuts and crisps

3 Your friend eats only fruit and yoghurt because he thinks this is healthy. Explain to him why he is wrong.

Talking and doing

4 Your class from college is going away for a week on a trip. You are going to stay in a hostel with a super kitchen. Each day, one group from the class has to make all the meals – breakfast, lunch and dinner (and perhaps something mid-morning or mid-afternoon if you are all hungry).

    a In groups, plan your meals for one day now. Use your dictionary or ask your teacher to help with difficult words and expressions.
    b Write up your day's menu and explain it to the class.
    c Which group do you all think has the nicest menu?

Revision spot

Giving advice (You shouldn't, ought to, etc)

You **should eat** a lot of fresh vegetables.
You **ought to have** some dairy products every day, too.
It is a good idea to eat natural, not highly processed food.

You **shouldn't eat** too many crisps!

You **oughtn't to eat** too much sugar.
It is not a good idea to fry everything in a lot of fat.

Practice

Make sentences about staying healthy with the expressions above.

Example: Get some exercise (like walking or swimming) every day.
            You should get some exercise (like walking or swimming) every day.

    a Sit for hours and hours in front of the TV.
    b Work all the time.
    c Relax with friends and go out sometimes, too.
    d Go to the dentist at least once a year.
    e Tell a friend if you have a problem.
    f Walk or cycle when you can.
    g Travel by car all the time.
    h Think that you are perfect and never make mistakes.
    i Eat very little so that you are as thin as possible.
    j Smoke.

Can you think of two more tips yourself?

Unit 6 Staying healthy

The work of a dietician

> The care workers who specialize in diet and nutrition are dieticians. Kim Lee Chan is one of these. This is her work.

While reading **1** Kim Lee helps patients, of course, but she also often helps other care workers. Find an example in the text of where she works with a social worker. How did she help her?

'I am a dietician. It is my job to know about food – the normal healthy food that everyone needs every day, and the special food which some people sometimes need.

Dieticians work in many different places and with many different kinds of people. Some work with big food manufacturers, some in homes for older people, some with sports- men and women, others in schools and factories where they prepare food.

I work in a hospital and am in charge of a team of dieticians. I look after the patients in the hospital, and the people (called 'out-patients') who come to see us there with special problems.

In the hospital, I give advice about the food which we prepare for the patients. I also see patients who need a special diet – for example, after a heart attack. Much of my job is like teaching: I have to tell people how their life may now change, how they will need different food, and help them to make the changes.

The out-patients who visit me at the hospital have many different kinds of problems. They may be diabetics, or have very high cholesterol. Often I see children who have allergies to different foods – they cannot drink milk, for example, or eat white bread. Again, my job is to explain and teach about a new diet.

56

Staying healthy Unit 6

People often have very funny old-fashioned ideas about food, and I have to tell them that most of these are wrong!

Because I am the expert in diet, doctors, nurses and many other care workers come to me for advice about the people that they are caring for. This morning, for example, I talked to a social worker about a family who are ill because they have a very bad diet, and I gave her some ideas for a better one.'

Patients often need special diets. Here, two dieticians in Kim Lee's team are preparing food in a hospital kitchen.

After reading 2 Answer these questions about the text.

a Why do you think that dieticians sometimes work in schools in Britain? (They do not usually teach children, so what is their job in the school?)
b In the hospital, Kim Lee has two different jobs. What are they?
c What is an 'out-patient'?
d Why is Kim Lee's job often 'like teaching'?
e What ideas do people often have about food according to Kim Lee?

Talking and doing 3 Talk about one of these questions in a group. Then tell the class your ideas.

a Why do sportsmen and women often need the help of a dictician? What kind of advice do you think that dieticians like Kim Lee can give them?
b You have just found out that from now on in your life there will be some foods that you can never eat! How difficult would you find this?
c Kim Lee says that this morning she spoke to a social worker about a family who are ill because their diet is bad. What could the reasons for this be? What ideas do you think Kim Lee perhaps gave the social worker?

57

Alcohol

Alcohol can be a factor in many different health and social problems. For young people between around 18 and 25 it can be particularly dangerous.

Before reading   **1** What has just happened in this picture? What do you think is happening now?

People like a drink with their friends, but drink-driving kills. The old advice is still the best: if you drink, don't drive, if you drive, don't drink.

You are at a party. It is the end of the evening and a friend offers to drive you home. You think he has been drinking alcohol. What do you do?
5 Going by car would be a lot quicker than taking the bus, and it is raining. But …
At the same party, another friend has also been drinking. She wants
10 to drive home in her car. What do you do?
You don't think it is a good idea, but she is your friend and you don't want an argument …
15 Drink-driving kills people – and not just the drivers themselves, but their friends who drive with them, and other people on the road.
In the USA, where most high school
20 students drive a car, drink-driving kills thousands of young people a year, and injures many thousands more. To try to change this situation, a well-known magazine organized
25 competitions for students and advertising companies to think of a poster: it went into high schools for students to see and they would, hopefully, think twice before they drove after
30 drinking, or drove with a drunk friend. You can see some of the posters on the next page.

Talking and doing   **2** Describe the posters on the next page. Which poster do you like best and why? Use these expressions:

The first poster shows …
On poster number two you can see …
The words on the poster are …
The third poster says …

3 In a group or with a partner either a) make your own poster and show it to the class or b) imagine that you are in one of the situations on page 58 (at the party). Write a short dialogue between the friends.

1

If you're going to drink and drive tonight, don't forget to kiss your mother goodbye.

3

Think twice when a drunk driver offers to take you with him.

2

Is one of your classmates going to kill you this year?

Don't drive drunk or ride with drunk driver.

4

ONE FOR THE ROAD.

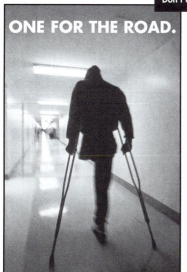

6

IF 4th HOUR ENGLISH SEEMS ENDLESS, TRY SITTING HERE FOR FIFTY YEARS.

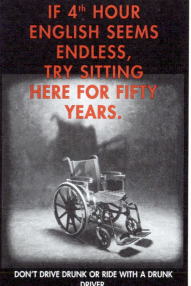

DON'T DRIVE DRUNK OR RIDE WITH A DRUNK DRIVER.

5

Think of your best friend.

Now, think of your best friend dead.

Don't drive drunk.

Unit 6   Staying healthy

'E' is for Ecstasy

Drugs can also kill – and it is not always easy for young people to say 'no' to them. This is a true story about one girl who took Ecstasy.

Before reading 1 Do you know the main danger for young people who take Ecstasy at a disco when they are dancing?

REAL LIFE DRAMAS

Karen thought taking E was just a bit of fun. But it soon took over her whole life.

'I first tried Ecstasy two years ago with my mate Lynn at a club. I took half a tablet called a 'white dove'. It was
5 amazing! I felt brilliant and happier than ever before. I loved everyone and everyone loved me too. I danced non-stop and it was the best
10 night I'd ever had.

From then on I took half an E whenever I went clubbing at weekends. I wasn't worried because I was a sens-
15 ible drug taker – I had my own flat and a job, I had read about the dangers and was always careful – I didn't buy from strangers, and
20 I remembered to drink water so I didn't become dehydrated.

The trouble started after three or four months. I
25 began to feel very depressed when I wasn't on E, I could not sleep and didn't get up for work. One afternoon, my boss called me into his office
30 for a 'chat'. I said I was OK, but my work got worse after that. Two months later I was sacked. A month after that I had a massive row with my
35 boyfriend and we split up. My flat was a complete mess, and I didn't pay my bills. The crazy thing is that I didn't think all this was anything to
40 do with drugs!

Unit 6

The final straw came one night when I bought a 'bad' tablet from a dealer I didn't know. I thought I was going to 45 die. I had heard about people dying from Ecstasy, but I didn't believe it would ever happen to me. Someone got me to a doctor. I expected a boring 50 lecture, but he was fantastic. After seeing him, I took a good look at my life. It took a long time, but now I've got a new job, and only go to clubs that 55 are drug-free. I wish I had never tried the stuff!'

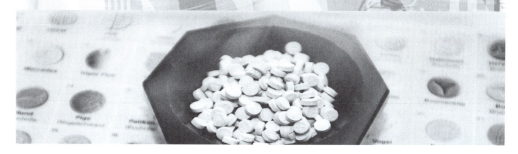

After reading 2 Answer these questions about the text.

a Why do you think Karen started to take Ecstasy regularly?
b Why did she not worry at first about taking it?
c How soon did the problems begin? Name some of the problems she had.
d One evening she had to see a doctor. Explain what happened.
e How did the doctor help her most, do you think?
f How does Karen feel about drugs now?

3 Explain these parts of the text in your own words.

a my mate Lynn (line 2)
b I loved everyone and everyone loved me (lines 6–8)
c I went clubbing at weekends (lines 12–13)
d I was a sensible drug taker (lines 14–15)
e (my boyfriend and I) split up (line 35)
f the final straw (line 41)
g I expected a boring lecture but he was fantastic (lines 49–50)
h I only go to clubs that are drug-free (lines 54–55)

Talking and doing 4 Malik Asubar (the Youth Worker from Unit 1) works with young people in the inner-city. He often has to talk to them about drugs. Work in a group. What can Malik say to the young people? Use Karen's story for ideas. Think about these questions.

a Why do people start taking drugs?
b Why is it hard 'to say no'?
c What problems can people have when they take drugs?
d What should they do not to begin taking drugs?
e What should they do if they already have a problem?

61

Vocabulary

Zeichenerklärung: ⚠ Achtung   ◄► Gegenteil   ≈ (ungefähr) gleichbedeutend mit

healthy	[ˈhelθi]	*gesund*
health	[helθ]	*Gesundheit*
pasta	[ˈpæstə]	*Nudeln*
carrot	[ˈkærət]	*Möhre*
cheese	[tʃiːz]	*Käse*
chicken	[ˈtʃɪkɪn]	*Hähnchen*
low in/high in	[ˈləʊ ɪn, ˈhaɪ ɪn]	*-arm/-reich*
fat	[fæt]	*fett*
salt	[sɔːlt]	*Salz*
fibre	[ˈfaɪbə]	*Ballaststoffe*
natural	[ˈnætʃrəl]	*natürlich*
		◄► **unnatural** – *unnatürlich*
highly processed	[ˌhaɪli ˈprəʊsest]	*stark konserviert*
balanced diet	[ˌbælənst ˈdaɪət]	*ausgewogene Diät*
starchy	[ˈstɑːtʃi]	*starkehältig*
carbohydrate	[ˌkɑːbəʊˈhaɪdreɪt]	*Kohlenhydrate*
rice	[raɪs]	*Reis*
cereals	[ˈsɪərɪəlz]	*Getreideprodukte*
dairy product	[ˈdeəri prɒdʌkt]	*Milchprodukt*
yoghurt	[ˈjɒgət]	*Joghurt*
meat alternative	[miːt ɔːlˈtɜːnətɪv]	*Fleischersatz*
pork	[pɔːk]	*Schweinefleisch*
lamb	[læm]	*Lamm(fleisch)*
beef	[biːf]	*Rindfleisch*
bean	[biːn]	*Bohne*
lentil	[ˈlentl]	*Linse*
nut	[nʌt]	*Nuss*
vegetable	[ˈvedʒtəbl]	*Gemüse*
fruit	[fruːt]	*Obst*
courgette	[kʊəˈʒet]	*Zucchini*
cabbage	[ˈkæbɪdʒ]	*Kohl*
salad	[ˈsæləd]	*Salat*
orange	[ˈɒrɪndʒ]	*Orange*
pear	[peə(r)]	*Birne*
to taste	[teɪst]	*schmecken*
horrible	[ˈhɒrəbl]	*entsetzlich*
peanut	[ˈpiːnʌt]	*Erdnuss*
crisps	[krɪsps]	*Kartoffelchips* ⚠ **chips** – *Pommes frites*
trip	[trɪp]	*Klassenfahrt*
menu	[ˈmenjuː]	*Speisekarte*
dietician	[ˌdaɪəˈtɪʃn]	*Diätist/in*
to specialize	[ˈspeʃəlaɪz]	*sich spezialisieren*
nutrition	[njuˈtrɪʃn]	*Ernährung*
kind (of)	[ˈkaɪnd əv]	*Art (von)*
manufacturer	[ˌmænjuˈfæktʃərə]	*Hersteller/in*

Vocabulary — Unit 6

sportsman	['spɔːtsmən]	Sportler
factory	['fæktəri]	Fabrik
out-patient	['aʊtpeɪʃnt]	ambulante/r Patient/in
problem	['prɒbləm]	Problem
heart attack	['hɑːt ətæk]	Herzinfarkt
diabetic	[ˌdaɪə'betɪk]	Diabetiker/in
cholesterol	[kə'lestərɒl]	Cholesterin
allergy	['ælədʒi]	Allergie ⚠ Aussprache
old-fashioned	[ˌəʊld'fæʃənd]	altmodisch
special diet	[ˌspeʃl 'daɪət]	Spezialdiät
reason	['riːzn]	Grund
to ride (with someone)	['raɪd wɪð]	mit jdm mitfahren ⚠ unregelmäßig
thousand	['θaʊznd]	tausend
to injure	['ɪndʒə]	verletzen
competition	[ˌkɒmpə'tɪʃn]	Wettbewerb
advertising company	['ædvətaɪzɪŋ kʌmpəni]	Werbeagentur
hopefully	['həʊpfli]	hoffentlich
to imagine	[ɪ'mædʒɪn]	sich vorstellen
dialogue	['daɪəlɒg]	Dialog
think twice	[θɪŋk 'twaɪs]	gründlich nachdenken ⚠ unregelmäßig
classmate	['klɑːsmeɪt]	Klassenkamerad/in
one for the road	[wʌn fə ðə 'rəʊd]	einen für den Heimweg trinken
Ecstasy	['ekstəsi]	Ecstasy (Droge)
danger	['deɪndʒə]	Gefahr
club	[klʌb]	Discothek
tablet	['tæblɪt]	Tablette
dove	[dʌv]	Taube
amazing	[ə'meɪzɪŋ]	erstaunlich
brilliant	['brɪliənt]	großartig
non-stop	[ˌnɒn'stɒp]	ohne aufzuhören
whenever	[wen'evə]	immer wenn
to go clubbing	[gəʊ 'klʌbɪŋ]	tanzen gehen ⚠ unregelmäßig
sensible	['sensəbl]	vernünftig ⚠ **sensitive** – empfindlich
stranger	['streɪndʒə]	Fremde/r
dehydrated	[ˌdiː'haɪdreɪtɪd]	dehydriert
depressed	[dɪ'prest]	deprimiert
chat	[tʃæt]	Unterhaltung
I was sacked	[aɪ wəz 'sækt]	ich wurde entlassen
massive row	['mæsɪv raʊ]	ein heftiger Streit
to split up	[ˌsplɪt 'ʌp]	sich voneinander trennen ⚠ unregelmäßig
a complete mess	[kəm'pliːt mes]	ein völliges Durcheinander
the final straw	[ðə faɪnl 'strɔː]	der Anstoß zum Umdenken
dealer	['diːlə]	Dealer/in
I expected a boring lecture	[aɪ ɪk'spektɪd ə ˌbɔːrɪŋ 'lektʃə]	ich erwartete eine langweilige Strafpredigt
stuff	[stʌf]	Zeug

7 Shop till you drop

Your household budget

Before reading   **1** What do you think the average family in countries like Britain and Germany spends the most money on? Put these four things in order, then read below to see if you were right.

a food
b housing (rent etc)
c leisure
d transport and communication (eg car/bus/phone)

Cards ('plastic money') are good for getting cash and paying for things when you want to.

Money! We all need it, and most of us hate organizing it! But every good home needs a household budget.

Rent, water, electricity, food, clothes, holidays … all have to be paid for, and nowadays there are a lot of good ways to plan your money. The bank
5 can help with monthly 'standing orders' so that you can pay your bills regularly; and cards of different kinds mean that you can always get cash, and pay for things when you want to.

So what do we spend all the money on? How the average family spends its money has changed a lot in the last 20 years. We spend much more
10 now than 20 years ago on leisure, but (in most countries) less on food – perhaps because we eat out more often now in restaurants. More people have cars and phones, so spending on those things is also higher. But we spend much less now than 20 years ago on tobacco.

The table on the next page shows how families in some European coun-
15 tries spend their money.

Shop till you drop   Unit 7

Household spending in percentages (some European countries)

	Germany	Britain	Austria	Sweden	Greece
Food	11	11	15	15	30
Alcohol and tobacco	4	9	4	5	7
Clothes	7	6	8	6	8
Things for the home (furniture etc)	8	7	8	7	7
Transport and communication	15	17	16	16	15
Housing (eg rent)	17	16	15	28	11
Fuel and power (gas, electricity etc)	3	4	4	5	2
Leisure	9	10	8	9	5
Health (eg medical insurance)	16	2	7	2	4
Other	10	18	15	7	11

After reading

2 Find the missing words in the text.

a *** *(Daueraufträge)* are a good way to pay your *** *(Rechnungen)* regularly.
b You can get *** *(Bargeld)* from a bank machine with a *** *(Karte)*.
c People *** *** *** *** *(geben ihr Geld für … aus)* many different things.
d People who live in a flat or house often have to pay *** *(Miete)*.
e The *** *** *(Durchschnittsfamilie)* spends more money now on leisure than it did 20 years ago.

3 Look at the table above and write five sentences about it. Use *more/less/the most/the least*.

Example: People in Austria spend **more** on food **than** people in Germany.
People in Britain spend **less** on clothes **than** people in Greece.
People in Greece spend **the most** on food, but **the least** on fuel and power.

4 With a partner, choose three statistics from the table which you find interesting, and try to think of the reasons for them.

Talking and doing

5 Work in a group. You all live together in a flat and have to pay all the usual bills. Your total budget each month (for all of you together) is shown in the table below. Altogether, you earn exactly €500 per month. In three months from now, you all want to go on holiday. It will cost €425. Plan your household budget for the next three months!

food	€55	rent	€85
alcohol and tobacco	€20	gas and electricity	€15
clothes	€35	leisure	€45
things for the home	€40	health insurance	€80
transport and phone	€75	other things	€50

Unit 7   Shop till you drop

What kind of shopper are you?

Supermarkets often use 'shopper-psychologists' to study how we shop.
One of these psychologists has put customers into six different categories.

While reading **1** Copy and fill in the table on page 67.

Mr Habit
Often an older person, Mr (or Mrs) Habit likes routines and always buys the same things – and if one of them is on 'special offer', that is even better.

John and Jilly
Are a young couple who both have good jobs and no kids. They like food, especially anything new and exotic, and spend a lot of money on it.

Ms Green
Ms (or Mr) Green is an idealist, who likes organic food and environmentally friendly products. She never spends much and the supermarkets do not really like her!

The Comfortables
The 'Comfortables' are young mothers, housewives or married couples with time and money. They like to buy 'nice' things, and Mrs Comfortable likes to get more than she needs – 'just to be sure'. The supermarkets love her!

Mrs Hectic
Mrs Hectic, on the other hand, has no time to shop. She has a busy job, and worse still, is often also a mother. She shops quickly, and likes to know where everything is in the store.

The Moneysavers
Mr and Mrs Moneysaver buy anything that is cheap, in large quantities if necessary. They may shop in one supermarket today, and another next week. Some have to do this because they are poor; others just hate spending money!

Name	Age	How much money do they spend?	How much time do they have to shop?	What is their main thought when shopping?
Mr Habit	×××	×××	×××	×××
John and Jilly	×××	×××	×××	×××
Ms Green	×××	×××	×××	×××

After reading 2 Look at the text and answer these questions.

   a What kind of shoppers do the supermarkets like most? Why?
   b What kind of shoppers do they like least? Why?
   c What kind of shoppers seem to enjoy shopping, and which probably hate it? Why?

Talking and doing 3 What kind of shopper are you? Is there a category here for you – or do you need a new one? Talk about your ideas in a group then tell the class.

Revision spot

Adjectives *(slow)* and adverbs of manner *(slowly)*

Mr and Mrs Comfortable are **slow** shoppers.
He is getting old and he is a bit **slow** now.
Mr and Mrs Comfortable shop **slowly**.

Practice

Choose the correct form of the word in brackets (adjective or adverb) for these sentences.

Example: The big supermarkets need to know how we shop. Some watch us very *carefully* (careful) with cameras while we are shopping.

   a They have identified a number of different types of shoppers. One – they call her 'Mrs Hectic' – shops very ××× (quick).
   b She has to be ××× (fast) because she is a mother who works all day, and when she shops, she often has her very ××× (bored) children with her.
   c 'The Moneysavers', on the other hand, like to look for ××× (cheap) products and they shop more ××× (slow).
   d 'John and Jilly' live very ××× (good). They like food – especially anything which is a bit ××× (exotic) and buy ××× (expensive) things.
   e Ms Green only buys things which are ××× (friendly) to the environment – ××× (organic) food, for example.
   f Mr Habit lives quite ××× (cheap). In the supermarket, he usually buys the same things every week and looks for ××× (special) offers.
   g The Comfortables are ××× (popular) with the supermarkets because they have time to shop. In fact, they like to do everything ××× (comfortable), so this is how they shop, too.

Unit 7   Shop till you drop

Know your rights

> When firms sell things, they must obey laws.
> These laws are there to help you – the buyer – and if you
> are not happy, you can complain.

While reading   **1**   Here are some examples of people who were not happy with what they bought. Find the law or laws (on page 69) which could help them.

The superholiday that wasn't

Andy Richards booked a great holiday in Antigua. The brochure described the hotel as 'luxurious', but when Andy arrived he found the room was loud and dirty, the
5 food was terrible, and the swimming pool was closed. When he got back, he complained to the holiday firm but they only offered him a few pounds and said they were sorry. Andy was not happy!

Hugo's car

10 Hugo is a college student. The most important thing in his life is his car, a wonderful and very old 'Beetle'. Hugo can repair the car himself, but when he wanted it painted red last year he went to a garage which spe-
15 cialized in that kind of work. When Hugo fetched his car, it looked terrible! The red was not the same everywhere, and there was paint on one of the tyres. Hugo complained, and the garage agreed to paint the car again
20 – but wanted more money.

Lyn's bed

Lyn Evans needs a special bed after a sports accident, and a shop said they had one that would be 'perfect' for her. But when it arrived, she found it was much too soft and
25 hurt her back, so she phoned the manager. He agreed to change the bed and said Lyn could keep the old one until it came. Two days later, however, he phoned to say he would not change the bed after all, and
30 would not take the old bed back because Lyn had now slept in it.

Know Your Rights: The Laws

1 Things which you buy must be safe.
2 They must be of 'satisfactory quality' – for example, if you buy a pair of jeans, the buttons must not fall off when you put them on!
3 They must do what the firm says they do – for example, computer software for one kind of computer, must work on that computer.
4 They must be 'as described' – for example, if a firm says that a car is 'new', it has to be new.
5 When firms do things for you, they must do them properly – if someone repairs your TV, it must work afterwards.
6 Firms must do the things 'in a reasonable time' – if they say they will send you some CDs in three weeks, then they should not arrive six months later.
7 If you agree on a price for something before you begin – for example, the cost of painting your house – the firm must keep to that price. If you do not agree before you begin, then the price must be 'reasonable' – in other words, they cannot suddenly ask you for millions of marks!
8 A firm must do what it agrees to do in a contract – even if the agreement is only 'verbal' (for example, on the telephone).

After reading 2 What are the missing words?

a Firms which sell to customers have to obey ✱✱✱ (Gesetze).
b If a buyer is not happy, he or she can ✱✱✱ (sich klagen).
c You should always ✱✱✱ (einen Preis vereinbaren) before you hire a firm to do work for you.
d Clothes which you buy must be ✱✱✱ (von passender Qualität).
e Goods must be ✱✱✱ (wie beschrieben).
f A ✱✱✱ (Vertrag) is an agreement between two people.

Talking and doing 3 Answer one of these questions.

a Think of another example of an unhappy buyer, like those on page 68. Write a short text and read it to the class. Get them to find the law or laws which could help the buyer.
b Has something like this ever happened to you – or a friend or someone in your family? Prepare a short talk about it for the class.

> **Useful phrases**
>
> This happened two years ago/last year/last week …
> I/Mr Smith/a friend of mine/my sister bought/hired/booked/
>   asked (someone to do something) …
> When we got home/a week later/afterwards, he/we) found that …
> (The goods) were dirty/broken/torn/too small/not satisfactory …
> They did not work/we could not operate them/(it) was awful …
> First/then/next/after that/finally …
> He/we complained about/asked about …
> They said that/told us that …
> They refused to/agreed to …
> In the end …

Advertising

It is no good having the best product in the world if no one knows about it, so firms try to sell us their products with advertisements. And how they do it is often very clever.

Shop till you drop   Unit 7

While reading 1 Answer the questions about these two advertisements.

a Describe what you see in each advertisement.
b What product is each one selling?
c Who do you think will buy the products? (Older people? Men? …). Explain your answer.
d Give the name of a newspaper or magazine in your country that might have advertisements like these (in German, of course!). Explain your answer.
e Now explain how the advertisements try to sell you the product.

> **Useful expressions**
>
> The first/second advertisement shows …
> It is surprising/amusing …
> The dog/the people are sad/bored/boring …
> The advertisement makes you think that …
> It makes you laugh/feel sorry for …
> I can identify with (the person in the picture) …

Talking and doing 2 Which advertisement do you like better? Why?

3 Now you are an advertiser! Work in a group. Choose one of the products below (or another one if you prefer) and make an advert for it. Then present it to the class.

Remember: Who will buy it? Will people look at and remember your advertisement?

Vocabulary

Zeichenerklärung: ⚠ Achtung

shop till you drop	[ʃɒp tɪl ju 'drɒp]	einkaufen bis zum Umfallen
household budget	[ˌhaʊshəʊld 'bʌdʒɪt]	Haushaltsgeld
average	['ævərɪdʒ]	Durchschnitts-
to spend money on	[spend 'mʌni ɒn]	Geld ausgeben für ⚠ unregelmäßig
housing	['haʊzɪŋ]	Wohnungen
rent	[rent]	Miete
leisure	['leʒə]	Freizeit
communication	[kəˌmjuːnɪ'keɪʃn]	Kommunikation
to organize	['ɔːgənaɪz]	organisieren
monthly	['mʌnθli]	monatlich
standing order	[ˌstændɪŋ 'ɔːdə]	Dauerauftrag
bill	[bɪl]	Rechnung
card	[kɑːd]	Karte
cash	[kæʃ]	Bargeld
restaurant	['restrɒnt]	Restaurant ⚠ Aussprache
spending	['spendɪŋ]	Ausgaben
tobacco	[tə'bækəʊ]	Tabak
percentage	[pə'sentɪdʒ]	Prozentsatz
Austria	['ɒstriə]	Österreich
Sweden	['swiːdn]	Schweden
power	['paʊə]	Strom
medical insurance	[ˌmedɪkl ɪn'ʃʊərəns]	Krankenversicherung
usual	['juːʒuəl]	üblich
exactly	[ɪg'zæktli]	genau
shopper	['ʃɒpə]	Käufer/in
category(-ies)	['kætəgəri]	Kategorie
habit	['hæbɪt]	Gewohnheit
(on) special offer	[ɒn ˌspeʃl 'ɒfə]	(im) Sonderangebot
couple	['kʌpl]	Paar
exotic	[ɪg'zɒtɪk]	exotisch
Ms	[mɪz]	Frau
idealist	[aɪ'dɪəlɪst]	Idealist/in
organic food	[ɔːˌgænɪk 'fuːd]	Bio-Produkte
environmentally friendly	[ɪnˌvaɪrən'mentəli 'frendli]	umweltfreundlich
married couple	[ˌmærɪd 'kʌpl]	Ehepaar
just to be sure	[dʒʌst tə bi 'ʃʊə]	um ganz sicher zu sein
hectic	['hektɪk]	hektisch
store	[stɔː]	Laden
moneysaver	['mʌniseɪvə]	Sparer/in
in large quantities	[ɪn lɑːdʒ 'kwɒntətiz]	in großen Mengen
adverb of manner	[ˌædvɜːb əv 'mænə]	Adverb der Art und Weise
in brackets	[ɪn 'brækɪts]	in Klammern
to identify	[aɪ'dentɪfaɪ]	identifizieren

Vocabulary — Unit 7

bored	[bɔ:d]	*gelangweilt*
to obey laws	[ə'beɪ lɔ:z]	*die Gesetze einhalten*
to complain	[kəm'pleɪn]	*(sich) beschweren*
superholiday	[ˌsu:pə'hɒlədeɪ]	*Superurlaub*
luxurious	[lʌg'ʒʊəriəs]	*luxuriös*
loud	[laʊd]	*laut*
closed	[kləʊzd]	*geschlossen*
soft	[sɒft]	*weich*
to hurt	[hɜ:t]	*wehtun* ⚠ unregelmäßig
safe	[seɪf]	*sicher*
(of) satisfactory quality	[əv ˌsætɪs'fæktəri kwɒləti]	*von zufriedenstellender Qualität*
pair of jeans	[ə peər əv 'dʒi:nz]	*eine Jeans*
button	['bʌtn]	*Knopf*
to repair	[rɪ'peə]	*reparieren*
to work (= to function)	[wɜ:k]	*funktionieren*
as described	[əz dɪ'skraɪbd]	*wie beschrieben*
afterwards	['ɑ:ftəwədz]	*danach*
reasonable	['ri:znəbl]	*vernünftig*
contract	['kɒntrækt]	*Vertrag*
agreement	[ə'gri:mənt]	*Vereinbarung*
verbal	['vɜ:bl]	*mündlich*
goods	[gʊdz]	*Güter*
torn	[tɔ:n]	*zerrissen*
advertising	['ædvətaɪzɪŋ]	*Werbung*
advertisement	[əd'vɜ:tɪsmənt]	*Werbung*
to wake up	[ˌweɪk 'ʌp]	*aufwachen*
a faceful of spots	['feɪsfəl əv spɒts]	*ein Gesicht voller Pickel*
rough side	[ˌrʌf 'saɪd]	*rauhe Seite*
to clear	[klɪə]	*entfernen*
skin	[skɪn]	*Haut*
grease	[gri:s]	*Fett*
grime	[graɪm]	*Schmutz*
pore	[pɔ:]	*Pore* ⚠ Aussprache
bacteria	[bæk'tɪəriə]	*Bakterien*
to cause	[kɔ:z]	*verursachen*
to wipe out	[ˌwaɪp 'aʊt]	*abtöten*
medicated smooth side	['medɪkeɪtɪd smu:ð saɪd]	*medizinisch behandelte weiche Seite*
Oxycute	['ɒksɪkju:t]	*Wortspiel = **execute** (töten)*
choosy	['tʃu:zi]	*wählerisch*
salmon	['sæmən]	*Lachs*
amusing	[ə'mju:zɪŋ]	*lustig*
to make (someone do something)	[meɪk 'du:]	*veranlassen* ⚠ unregelmäßig
to feel sorry for (someone)	[fi:l 'sɒri fə]	*jdn bemitleiden* ⚠ unregelmäßig
to identify (with)	[aɪ'dentɪfaɪ]	*sich mit jdm/etw identifizieren*
advertiser	['ædvətaɪzə]	*Werbefachmann/frau*
advert	['ædvɜ:t]	*Werbung*

8 Caring for the environment

The world in which we live

Our environment affects everyone. But it is particularly important for homemakers and care workers to be 'good citizens'. This means knowing about the world in which we live.

While reading   **1**   Read the text below and answer these questions with a partner.

    a Which gas causes global warming? Where does this gas come from?
    b Give two reasons why cutting down rainforests is bad for the environment.
    c Why are so many species of animals lost every day?
    d Give two reasons why throwing away so much rubbish is bad for the environment.
    e 'We waste water because we use so much for eating and drinking every day.' Is this statement true or false?
    f Which countries in the world are mainly responsible for the energy crisis? Why?
    g What alternatives are there to coal and oil for energy? Which seem to be better? Why?
    h Why could it be dangerous to sit too long in the sun on holiday? What has caused this problem?

Our environment: some important facts

1 Global warming

Global warming is caused by the gases, mainly carbon dioxide, from cars and power stations which produce electricity. Because of it, the world's climate is changing. In Europe, each family is responsible for around 20 tonnes of the gas each year. Each litre of petrol in a car gives off around 2 kg of it!

Too many cars cause pollution, so be nice to the world – use your bike!

2 Rainforests

We are cutting down rainforests so fast that many people believe that by the year 2030 they will all be gone. People, animals and plants live there – but the rainforests also give us around a quarter of all our oxygen. Cutting them down is making global warming much worse. We are creating problems for our children tomorrow.

3 Waste

Each family in Europe produces about 10–15 kg of rubbish every week. A lot could be recycled. Rubbish gets into the earth and the water and pollutes it, and it takes more energy to produce the goods again. As well as wasting things, we also waste water. Each person in Europe uses around 150 litres of it a day – only three litres of which is for eating and drinking!

4 Killing animals and plants

We all need food, but plants and animals are often killed for nothing – or for money or for fun. Every day, around 50 species of plants and animals are lost for ever! The sooner we all realise this, the better.

5 Energy

The USA and Europe use four times as much energy as countries like Africa or South America. We are using up coal and oil fast – and polluting the air. Nuclear energy is cleaner – but it has many dangers, too. Many people want to look at energy from the sun, water and the wind as alternatives.

6 Ozone

It is no longer safe to sit for too long in the sun on holiday because there are holes in the 'ozone layer' around the earth. Ozone is destroyed by CFCs which come from fridges, some kinds of packaging and spray cans.

Unit 8 Caring for the environment

The environment and your home

> So how can we be 'good citizens' in the home?
> Here are two couples – the Whites and the Blacks.
> Both do some things right, but some things wrong.

Before reading **1** Recycling paper is a 'good' thing – but using too much electricity is 'bad'. Can you think of one more 'good' thing and one more 'bad' thing?

The Whites

Henry and Paula White live in the country where there isn't a good bus service, so they have a car. However, their car is small and they use it as little as possible.
5 For example, they shop just once a week in the supermarket in town.

The Whites live in an old cottage, but it is modern and most important of all well-insulated. They are careful about
10 switching off lights but Henry often leaves his computer on even when he is not using it. Because they are so busy all week, Henry and Paula have a dishwasher. And Paula hates dirty clothes, so
15 she washes every day and of course uses her new washing machine.

The Whites regularly take all their old glass, paper and metal cans to the big recycling banks in the village. Henry hates too much paper and plastic. He gets angry in shops when things are wrapped in too much of
20 them. He takes it off or does not buy things wrapped like this! He thinks it would be much better if shoppers could leave all the paper and plastic wrapping in the shops for them to recycle.

The Blacks

Mary and Philip Black live and work in town. Mary is a teacher and goes to work every day on her bike, but Philip is a bit lazy: he often uses
25 their car.

When they go shopping, the Blacks always try to buy things like recycled paper products and organic vegetables. Mary takes a shopping bag so she does not need to get plastic bags from the shop. They are also very careful about their rubbish. Like the Whites, they take their old news-
30 papers, clothes, cans and bottles to the recycling banks in town.

76

Caring for the environment   **Unit 8**

After a busy day, Mary takes a shower. Philip likes to relax in a deep, hot bath. In the evenings, Mary watches TV, listens to
35 music, or reads – and often all three at the same time! The Blacks are always careful about their central heating. They keep it turned down and if the room
40 is a little cool, they just put on a pullover. 'Heat is money,' says Philip. 'This way our electricity bills are much lower.'

After reading   2   Here are some things that the Whites do. Look at each one and say if it is good or bad for the environment and explain why.

a The have a small car and use it as little as possible.
b Their cottage is well-insulated.
c Henry often leaves his computer on.
d They have a dishwasher.
e Paula washes clothes every day.
f They take their old glass to the bottle banks in the village.
g Henry does not buy things in shops that are wrapped in too much plastic.

3   Now look at the text about the Blacks. Make two lists: one of the good things that they do and one of the bad.

Talking and doing   4   How 'green' are you? Work in a group. Make a list together of the things that you do every day that are good for the environment, and another of the things that you do wrong. Would you say that you are a 'green' person?

Unit 8   Caring for the environment

Helping others to understand

Caring for the environment yourself is important, and you know what the good and bad things are. But one day, as a care worker or as a parent, you will have to help other people to understand, too. Particularly children need to learn what is good and bad for the environment.

Talking and doing

1 Look at this poster and discuss it. What does it show? What is it trying to say? Is it clear? Could young children understand it easily? Why (not)?

2 Imagine you are a teacher! You have a class of young children and want to teach them about the environment.
Choose one of the aspects of the environment that you have read about so far and design your own poster.

3 A short science fiction story can be a great way to interest people. Could you finish this one? Work in pairs.

The New World

The Starship Rubbish Bin is deep in space. On it, are the men and women of a world that is now dead. They are looking for a New World, a planet where they can begin a new life.

One day they find one which is perfect – green, with clean air and water, and filled with birds animals and plants.

At first, life on the New World (which they call 'Earth') is good. They have everything that they need, and they spend all day sitting in the sun eating the wild fruit. At night, there is wood in the forests for fires. But soon, this is not enough. They want to have all the machines which they had on their old planet …

Revision spot

The passive

Global warming **is caused by** gases from cars and power stations.
Thousands of animals **are killed** every day to sell parts of their bodies.

The passive is formed with **to be** + past participle (+ **by**).

Practice

Write these active sentences again as passive ones. Use *by* when it is necessary.

Example: Each litre of petrol gives off two kilograms of gas.
  Two kilograms of gas *are given* off *by* each litre of petrol.

a CFCs from fridges and spray cans cause holes in the ozone layer.
b Power stations produce a lot of the pollution in our world.
c People in countries like Holland use bikes all the time.
d A nuclear power station at Chernobyl caused a terrible accident in 1986.
e The pollution from Chernobyl destroyed thousands of hectares of land.
f If we are not careful, people will cut down more and more of the rainforests in the next 20 years.
g We are using up our coal and oil very quickly.
h We only use about three litres of water every day for eating and drinking. We mostly waste the other 147 litres.
i The rubbish which we throw away has polluted our earth and water.
j We could recycle most of our rubbish.

Unit 8 Caring for the environment

A different kind of care worker

> Care workers normally care for people.
> But Valerie Seldon is a care worker of a different kind.
> Her job is to care for the environment.
> This is an interview with her.

Before reading **1** What is happening in this picture? What do you think a 'nature garden' is?

Caring for the environment: Valerie Seldon with children in a 'nature garden' in the inner-city

Interviewer Valerie, how did you come to do the work that you're doing now?

Valerie I studied horticulture – that's flowers and gardening – at college and got very interested in the environment. I began working for the Wildlife Trust as a volunteer while I was at college. When I finished, I got a full-time job with them.

Interviewer And how long have you been working full-time now?

Valerie Just over two years.

Interviewer What is the Wildlife Trust?

Valerie The Wildlife Trust is a big national organization that tries to protect the environment. In lots of big cities, it has groups which teach people about the environment, try to make new flats look nicer, make 'nature gardens' on old land, that sort of thing. I'm a full-time worker, but most of the people in the trust are volunteers – they just do it because they like it.

Interviewer So, how do you make a nature garden?

Valerie Well, first we find or buy a piece of empty land. Often, there's a bit of a battle because someone wants to build offices on it! Then we work with the local people, and the schools, to clean up the land and make room for natural plants and flowers and animals to live here. The kids from the schools come here a lot. They love it.

Interviewer How long do you work each day?

Valerie My hours are supposed to be 9.30 to 5.30, but I'm nearly always here until much later. Yesterday I finished at 11 pm and I'm working this Saturday, too. Once the local people get interested, they want to see the garden as quickly as possible.

Interviewer It sounds as if this isn't just a 'job' for you.

Valerie No, it's much more than that. To do this, you really have to want to change the world!

After reading 2 True or false? If false, give a true statement.

a Valerie has worked full-time for the Wildlife Trust since she left college just over two years ago.
b All the people who work for the Trust are full-time workers like Valerie.
c It is always easy to get land for a nature garden.
d The local people and local schools help to make the gardens.
e Valerie works from 9.30 until 5.30 each day.
f The work is not really a job for Valerie because she does not get paid for it.

Talking and doing 3 Hackney is a poor area of London, with pieces of empty, dirty land, and blocks of flats. Valerie and the Wildlife Trust have just made a nature garden there. You are a reporter for the Hackney Post, the local newspaper. In a group, or with a partner, write an article for the paper. Think about the following questions and include interviews with Valerie and some of the local people.

a What was the piece of land before it became a garden?
b How did the Wildlife Trust get the land?
c How long did it take to make the garden?
d Who helped?
e What do they think of it now and how do they use it?

Vocabulary

Zeichenerklärung: ⚠ Achtung   ◀▶ Gegenteil   ≈ (ungefähr) gleichbedeutend mit

citizen	['sɪtɪzn]	(Staats-)Bürger/in
to mean	[mi:n]	*bedeuten* ⚠ unregelmäßig
global warming	[ˌgləʊbl 'wɔːmɪŋ]	*Erwärmung der Erdatmosphäre*
to cut down	[ˌkʌt 'daʊn]	*fällen (Baum)* ⚠ unregelmäßig
rainforest	['reɪnfɒrɪst]	*Regenwald*
species	['spiːʃiːz]	*Art* Plural: bleibt unverändert
to be lost	[bi 'lɒst]	*aussterben* ⚠ unregelmäßig
to throw away	[ˌθrəʊ ə'weɪ]	*wegwerfen* ⚠ unregelmäßig
rubbish	['rʌbɪʃ]	*Müll*
responsible (for)	[rɪ'spɒnsəbl fɔː]	*verantwortlich für*
crisis	['kraɪsɪs]	*Krise*
alternative	[ɔːl'tɜːnətɪv]	*Alternative* ⚠ Aussprache
coal	[kəʊl]	*Kohle*
power station	['paʊə ˌsteɪʃn]	*Kraftwerk*
climate	['klaɪmət]	*Klima*
tonne	[tʌn]	*Tonne* ⚠ Aussprache
litre	['liːtə]	*Liter*
plant	[plɑːnt]	*Pflanze* sonst auch Verb: *pflanzen*
oxygen	['ɒksɪdʒən]	*Sauerstoff*
worse	[wɜːs]	*schlimmer* ◀▶ **better** – *besser*
to produce	[prə'djuːs]	*produzieren*
to be recycled	[bi rɪ'saɪkld]	*wiederverwendet werden* ⚠ unregelmäßig
to pollute	[pə'luːt]	*verschmutzen* vgl. Nomen: **pollution** – *Verschmutzung*
to waste	[weɪst]	*verschwenden* sonst auch Nomen: *Verschwendung*
Africa	['æfrɪkə]	*Afrika*
nuclear energy	[ˌnjuːkliə 'enədʒi]	*Kernenergie*
wind	[wɪnd]	*Wind*
no longer	[nəʊ 'lɒŋgə]	*nicht mehr* He ~ lives here.
hole	[həʊl]	*Loch*
to destroy	[dɪ'strɔɪ]	*zerstören* vgl. Adjektiv: **destructive** – *zerstörerisch*
CFC	[ˌsiː ef 'siː]	*FCKW*
packaging	['pækɪdʒɪŋ]	*Verpackung*
spray can	['spreɪ kæn]	*Sprühdose*
cottage	['kɒtɪdʒ]	*Häuschen*
well-insulated	[ˌwel'ɪnsjuleɪtɪd]	*gut isoliert*

to switch (on/off)	[ˌswɪtʃ 'ɒn, ˌswɪtʃ ɒf]	ein-/ausschalten
		≈ **to turn (on/off)**
bin	[bɪn]	*Mülltonne*
to wrap (something in)	[ˌræp 'ɪn]	*verpacken*
colleague	['kɒliːg]	*Kollege, Kollegin*
recycled paper	[ˌriːˈsaɪkld peɪpə]	*Umweltpapier*
organic vegetables	[ɔːˌgænɪk 'vedʒtəblz]	*Biogemüse*
shopping bag	['ʃɒpɪŋ bæg]	*Einkaufstasche*
newspaper	['njuːspeɪpə]	*Zeitung*
to relax	[rɪˈlæks]	*sich entspannen*
		vgl Nomen: **relaxation** – *Entspannung*
deep	[diːp]	*tief*
		◀▶ **shallow** – *flach*
to turn (up/down)	[ˌtɜːn 'ʌp, ˌtɜːn 'daʊn]	*auf-/abdrehen*
		⚠ **switch (on/off)** aber nicht **(up/down)**
cool	[kuːl]	*kühl*
electricity bill	[ɪˌlektrɪsəti bɪl]	*Stromrechnung*
journey	['dʒɜːni]	*Fahrt*
idea	[aɪˈdɪə]	*Idee*
		No ~ – *Keine Ahnung*
poster	['pəʊstə]	*Plakat*
science fiction story	[ˌsaɪəns 'fɪkʃn stɔːri]	*Science-Fiction-Geschichte*
Starship Rubbish Bin	[ˌstɑːʃɪp 'rʌbɪʃ bɪn]	*Starship Mülleimer*
planet	['plænɪt]	*Planet* ⚠ *Aussprache*
wild fruit	[waɪld 'fruːt]	*Wildfrucht*
wood	[wʊd]	*Holz*
		vgl Adjektiv: **wooden** – *Holz-*
forest	['fɒrɪst]	*Wald*
machine	[məˈʃiːn]	*Maschine*
passive	['pæsɪv]	*Passiv*
Holland	['hɒlənd]	*Holland* ⚠ *Aussprache*
hectare	['hekteə]	*Hektar*
nature garden	['neɪtʃə gɑːdn]	*Naturschutzgarten*
horticulture	['hɔːtɪkʌltʃə]	*Gartenbau*
flower	['flaʊə]	*Blume*
gardening	['gɑːdnɪŋ]	*Gartenarbeit*
		vgl: Nomen: **gardener** – *Gärtner/in*
trust	[trʌst]	*Stiftung*
national organization	[ˌnæʃnəl ˌɔːgənaɪˈzeɪʃn]	*landesweite Organisation*
to protect	[prəˈtekt]	*schützen*
		vgl: Nomen: **protection** – *Schutz*
a piece of land	[ə 'piːs əv lænd]	*Grundstück*
there's a bit of a battle	[ðəz ə ˌbɪt əv ə 'bætl]	*es gibt einen ziemlichen Kampf*
are supposed to be	[səˈpəʊzd tə bi]	*sollten eigentlich sein*
local people	[ˌləʊkl 'piːpl]	*Ortsansässige*

Wordfield A — Care workers and their jobs

Words and expressions

Care workers
nurse, social worker, teacher, community nurse, hostel warden, youth (social) worker, child protection officer, 'carer', care assistant, dietician, a professional, a volunteer (worker), Samaritan, doctor, environmental worker

Where they work
hospital, clinic, hostel, (residential) home, in the community, in the inner-city

Care workers' jobs
to care for (people), to help (people with washing, dressing/to eat, to put on their make-up), to run (clubs, clinics), to visit (people at home), to protect (children), to look after (someone who is old), to give (people) advice

They care for
young people, older people, disabled people, abused children, people who are ill, people with problems, people who are lonely, homeless people, patients

The work
can be difficult, is satisfying, you have to be able to work in a team, you need a sense of humour, you have to understand that everyone is a person, you have to be kind and patient, can be full-time or part-time

Exercise 1 Use the words and expressions from the box to complete the sentences.

a Nurses are care workers. They sometimes work in a *** (Krankenhaus) and sometimes in the *** (Gemeinde).
b Some care workers are full-time professionals; others work *** (teilzeit) or are *** (Freiwillige).
c Some people who are older or *** (behindert) live in *** (Wohnheimen).
d *** (SozialarbeiterInnen) help people who are *** (heimatlos), or have other personal *** (Probleme). Some work with *** (Jugendliche); many work in the *** (Innenstadt).
e Care work can be very difficult, but care workers always say that it is very *** (befriedigend).

Exercise 2 Choose words and expressions from the box to continue. Write two or three sentences for each.

a Care workers ***
b Some examples of care workers are ***
c A typical care worker is ***. He or she ***
d To be a care worker you have to ***

Exercise 3 Complete this text about 'A day in the ward' *(Station)* in a hospital with words from this list. What do the words mean in German?

visiting time ∗ beds ∗ X-ray ∗ tablets ∗ operating theatre ∗ ward ∗ chart ∗ diet ∗ medicines ∗ temperature ∗ patients ∗ examines

A day in the ward

The day begins early when the night nurse wakes the patients. He or she takes their (1) ∗∗∗ and pulse and writes them on to a (2) ∗∗∗ which hangs at the end of the bed. Then the patients are washed and at about 8 am the day nurses arrive.

The patients can now have their breakfast. The nurses make their (3) ∗∗∗, then during the morning the doctor comes round and (4) ∗∗∗ the patients. Also during the morning, some of the patients may have to go to the (5) ∗∗∗ or for an (6) ∗∗∗.

The patients have their lunch at about 12 o'clock. Some may need a special (7) ∗∗∗, and so get different food from the others.

After lunch, it is (8) ∗∗∗ when

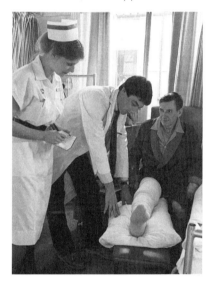

friends and relatives come. They often ask the nurses questions.

When the visitors have gone, many patients get up, walk around, read or talk. Hospitals like patients to get up and be active as soon as they can.

It is now evening. Before supper, the nurses bring round (9) ∗∗∗ and (10) ∗∗∗ for the patients, and write notes for the night nurses. The patients eat, chat, and watch television, then at about 22.30 the night nurse turns down the lights and watches the (11) ∗∗∗ while the (12) ∗∗∗ go to sleep. Tomorrow will be another day …

Wordfield B — People and relationships

Words and expressions

People
person, people, young people, older/elderly people, friend, relative, partner, boyfriend (girlfriend)

Verbs
to be born, to grow up, to get old, to die, to get married, to have children, to look after (someone)

Families
child(-ren), kid *(Umgangssprache)*, teenager, parent, mother, father, brother, sister, nuclear family, extended family, single-parent family, stepfamily, stepfather, stepmother, couple

Relationships
to fall in love with someone, to live with someone, to get on well with someone, to argue with someone, to have arguments with someone, to agree/disagree with someone, to be jealous (of someone), to like someone, to not like someone very much

People can be
nice, kind, friendly, unfriendly, difficult, bad-tempered, tidy, untidy, tired, lazy, happy, unhappy, difficult, forgetful, thoughtful, excited, bored, crazy

Exercise 1 Use the words and expressions from the box to complete the sentences.

a Jenny is ××× *(eine nette Person)*.
b But her sisters Melanie and Rachel are not very ××× *(nette Leute)*.
c We all ××× *(aufwachsen)*, ××× *(alt werden)*, and ××× *(sterben)*.
d Many people ××× *(heiraten)* but many also just live with a ××× *(Partner)*.
e ××× *(Alleinerziehende)* are families where a mother or father brings up a ××× *(Kind)* or ××× *(Kinder)* alone.
f If two people ××× (heiraten) who were married before, and if they have children, then this makes a kind of family called a ××× *(Stieffamilie)*.
g Most young people ××× *(kommen gut mit … aus)* their parents. But, of course, they sometimes ××× *(streiten)* with them, too.
h The opposite of 'friendly' is ××× and the opposite of 'easy' is ×××.

Exercise 2 Choose words and expressions from the box to continue.

a I like people who are ×××
b I don't like people very much who are ×××
c Two people fall in love then they ×××
d It is not always possible to ×××

Exercise 3 Look at this family tree and complete the sentences. Use these words.

aunt ('auntie') * brother * brother-in-law * children * cousin * cousins * daughter * family * grandchildren * grandfather ('grandad') * grandmother ('granny') * husband * married * nephew * niece * relatives * sister * sister-in-law * sons * uncle * wife

a Bill and Ethel had two (1) ×××: David and Helen.
b David and Helen are now both (2) ×××: David's (3) ××× is called Susan and Helen's (4) ××× is called Peter.
c David and Susan have two (5) ×××: Jason and Tim.
d Helen and Peter have a (6) ×××: Vicky.
e Jason, Tim and Vicky are Bill and Ethel's (7) ×××.
f Bill is Vicky's (8) ×××, and Ethel is her (9) ×××.
g Helen is David's (10) ×××, and David is her (11) ×××.
h Peter is David's (12) ×××. Susan is Helen's (13) ×××.
i David is Vicky's (14) ×××, and Susan is her (15) ×××.
j Vicky has two (16) ×××: Jason and Tim. Jason and Tim have just one (17) ××× – Vicky.
k Vicky is David's (18) ×××. Tim is Helen's (19) ×××.
l All these people are in the same (20) ×××, so they are all (21) ×××.

Wordfield C Health

Words and expressions

You can be
healthy, tired, ill, depressed

You may need
a doctor, a hospital, a dentist, a psychologist, a wheelchair, a stick, a holiday, a hobby, to relax, to get more exercise

In a hospital
you can be a patient, an out-patient

Because of ...
illness, an accident, an allergy, a heart attack, high cholesterol

Food
to stay healthy you need a healthy/balanced diet; food can be high in sugar, low in fat, salt or fibre; different kinds of food are carbohydrates, dairy products, meat, vegetables, fruit

It is not good
to smoke, to drink too much alcohol, to work all the time, to take drugs, to drink and drive

Exercise 1   Use the words and expressions from the box to complete the sentences.

a Mr Jones had to change his way of life after his ××× *(Herzinfarkt)*.
b A balanced diet includes some of these every day: ××× *(Kohlenhydrate)*, ××× *(Milchprodukte)*, ××× *(Fleisch)*, and ××× *(Obst)* or ××× *(Gemüse)*.
c After an ××× *(Unfall)* people sometimes need to use a ××× *(Rollstuhl)* or a ××× *(Gehstock)* for a time.
d It is important to do something in your free time to ××× *(sich entspannen)*. No one should work ××× *(die ganze Zeit)*.
e Only very stupid people ××× *(Drogen nehmen)*.

Exercise 2   With a partner, copy and complete this bubble diagram (part of it is done for you to show you how). Use words that you know, or look words up in your dictionary.

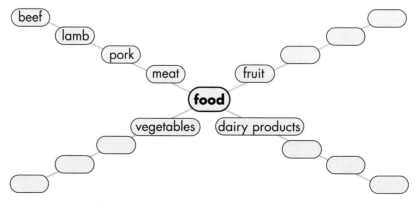

Exercise 3 Think of another bubble diagram yourself. It could be about:

a illness
b household activities
c health in general
d elderly people

Exercise 4 Look at the parts of the body. Match the numbers on the picture with the words in the list.

ear * neck * eyebrow * chest * stomach ('tummy') * shoulder * elbow * waist * wrist * thumb * mouth * head * face * breast * foot (feet) * knee * eye(s) * nose * bottom * tooth (teeth) * leg * hair * ankle

Wordfield D The home

Words and expressions

Types of homes
flat, house, block of flats, (residential) home, cottage

Rooms
your (own) room, kitchen, bathroom, living room, den (American English), bedroom, toilet

Things in the home
furniture, rug, sofa, door, window, bath(tub), shower, table, chair, cooker, dishwasher, washing machine, sink, worksurface (for working on in the kitchen), fridge, microwave

Housework
shopping, cooking, washing up, cleaning, washing (clothes), ironing, doing household repairs (DIY: Do It Yourself), paying bills, looking after children

Homes can be
tidy, untidy, small, large, modern, old, well-designed

Dangers in the home
you can fall over, cut yourself, get poisoned (by things), fall out (of windows), burn yourself, get an electric shock (from things)

Exercise 1

These sentences define words and expressions from the box above. What are they?

a An old, often small house in the country.
b Where you put food to keep it cool.
c The room where you sleep.
d What you pay. They come from the electricity, gas, water and telephone companies.
e This can happen if you drink some household chemicals.
f Chairs, tables, sofas and beds are all kinds of ✳✳✳.
g For cooking, modern kitchens have a microwave as well as a ✳✳✳.
h After the meal, you put the dirty dishes into a machine called a ✳✳✳!
i Where you work in the kitchen, eg to cut vegetables.
j What you can get if you put an electric fire into the bath!

Exercise 2

Which is the odd one out? Why?

Example: house, flat, <u>window</u>, cottage (All the others are types of homes.)

a kitchen, den, living room, shower
b chair, DIY, shopping, ironing
c tidy, sink, small, well-designed

Wordfields

Exercise 3 Write one sentence about each of these. Use words and expressions from the box.

    a modern homes
    b housework
    c dangers in the home
    d your dream house

Exercise 4 Look at this living room. Match the numbers on the picture with the words in the list. Use your dictionary if you need to.

ceiling × wall × picture × vase × fireplace × stairs × desk × chair × coffee table × sofa × cushion × window × stereo × speaker × television × bookcase × plant × armchair × remote control × wall unit

91

Wordfield E — Money and shopping

Words and expressions

Verbs
to spend money (on something), to pay for something, to pay a bill, to buy something, to save money, to sell something, to shop, to go shopping

You can spend it on
food, clothes, alcohol, leisure, your home, gas and electricity, transport and communication, rent, a car, a holiday

You need
a household budget, standing orders to pay your bills regularly, a card to get cash from a machine

People
customer, shopper, buyer, seller, advertiser

Goods can be
cheap, expensive, on special offer

The law says they must be
safe, of satisfactory quality, as described, of a reasonable price

Prices
the bed costs £100, the price of the bed is £100
100 = one/a hundred
215 = two hundred and fifteen
1,765 = one thousand seven hundred and sixty-five
£25 = twenty five pounds
£5.99 = five (pounds) ninety-nine (p)
£0.75 = seventy-five pence/p

Exercise 1

These sentences define words and expressions from the box above. What are they?

a To give money for something. When you buy goods in a shop you have to *** *** them.
b A person who buys something in a shop.
c How much something costs is its ***.
d When goods in a shop are cheap today they are on '*** ***'.
e The telephone company sends you a *** every month. It shows how much money you have to pay for your phone calls.
f The money that you have to pay for your flat or house. Most people pay their *** every month.
g The opposite of 'expensive'.

Exercise 2

Write one sentence about each of these.

a looking around shops
b the laws about goods
c a household budget
d your favourite shop

Wordfields

Exercise 3 Write down ten prices and say them to your partner. Can he or she write them down correctly? Compare your two lists afterwards.

Exercise 4 Look at these clothes. Match the numbers on the pictures with the words in the list.

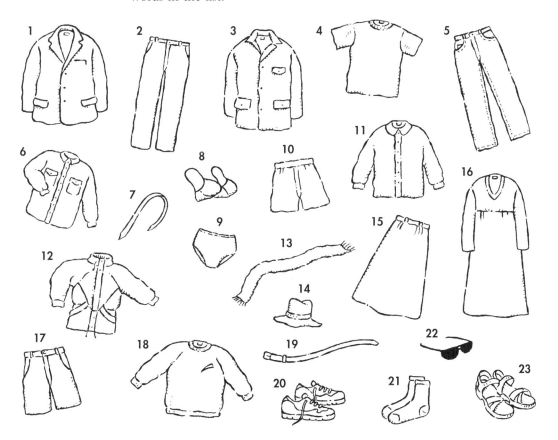

jacket * trousers * shirt * tie * leather jacket * T-shirt * jeans * winter jacket * belt * sweatshirt * shorts * socks * trainers * blouse * skirt * dress * sandals * hat * scarf * sunglasses * boxer shorts * pants/panties * bra

Exercise 5 Choose the correct word each time in brackets.

a How much *** (is/are) the sunglasses?
b The jacket *** (cost/costs) only twenty pounds but the trousers *** (cost/costs) over a hundred!
c You should buy *** (some/a) boxer shorts, Pete. *** (It/They) would look good on you.
d How much *** (do/does) the black jeans *** (cost/costs)?
e I spent a lot of money *** (on/for) clothes last week.
f This jacket is made *** (from/of) leather.
g Susan paid for her dress *** (by cheque/with a cheque).

Wordfield F — The environment

Words and expressions

The environment
can be clean, beautiful, healthy, dirty, polluted

We can
care for it, think about it, pollute it

At home
to use (your car, electricity), to save (energy), to waste (water), to throw away (paper), to recycle (rubbish), to switch on/off (lights), to drive (a car), to go by bus, to go by bike, to go on your bike, to turn up/down your heating, to repair, modern and well-insulated

World problems
global warming, to cause, gas(es), carbon dioxide, oxygen, (to change the) climate, rainforest, to cut down (trees), to be lost for ever, a species of plant/animal, to make something (much) worse, to kill (animals) for money, to use up (coal and oil), nuclear energy, (alternative) energy from the sun, ozone, ozone layer, CFCs, spray cans, packaging

It is a good idea to
take glass, paper and cans to bins for recycling, take your own shopping bag when you go to the shops, take a shower not a bath

Exercise 1

The missing words in the sentences are all from the box. Each means the opposite of the underlined word. What are the words? (There may be more than one answer.)

a In some places the environment is <u>dirty</u> but in others it is *clean*.
b Some people try to <u>save</u> energy at home but others *** it.
c You can <u>turn up</u> your heating in the winter, but you should *** it *** again in spring.
d Some people just <u>throw away</u> old newspapers but others try to *** them.
e We should <u>plant</u> more trees – not *** them ***.
f The oxygen from rainforests could <u>make</u> the climate <u>better</u>. When we destroy the forests we *** it ***.
g Some people try to <u>save</u> the lives of animals, others *** them.

Exercise 2

Find the pairs of words which belong together, eg *carbon dioxide*. Then write a sentence with each one, eg *Carbon dioxide is a gas*.

energy * up * throw * ozone * <u>carbon</u> * bus * global * can * warming * cut * away * nuclear * by * layer * spray * <u>dioxide</u> * down * use

Exercise 3 Use words from the list to complete the text below. What do the words mean in German?

breed × gorilla × rhinoceros × macaw × the wild × horn × extinct × feathers × endangered × zoos

Endangered species

Every day, fifty species of plants and animals are lost from our planet. The United Nations believes that by the middle of the 21st century, 25 per cent of all species could be (1) ×××, that is, gone for ever. We call these the (2) ××× species.

You can see some of the birds and animals which are in danger in the photos. One is the (3), ××× which lives in the mountains of Africa. Another is the black (4) ×××. Its (5) ××× is thought by some people in Asia to be a strong medicine, so they kill it in the same way that they kill elephants for their tusks.

Many animals are killed because they are beautiful – for their skin or (6) ×××. This is what is happening to a beautiful bird called the blue (7) ×××, which lives in the rainforests.

(8) ××× can sometimes save animals which are dying. This is what has happened with the Arabian oryx. It died out in 1972, but people now (9) ××× it in zoos and then re-introduce the animals into (10) ×××.

Quellenverzeichnis

Titel:
The Stock Market, Düsseldorf (Jon Feingersh/Tom & DeeAnn McCarthy, Ariel Skelley)

Fotos:
AGE Concern, London S. 26
Jim Austin, Berlin S. 44, 46, 47 (2), 71, 77
BAVARIA Bildagentur, Düsseldorf S. 7/ISP, 26/FPG, 28/VCL, 45/PP, 50/Thomas, 57/Images, 64/VCL, 75/TCL
Das Fotoarchiv, Essen S. 74/Mayer
Department for Education and Employment, Sheffield S. 11, 80
Deutscher Blindenverband e.V., Berlin S. 10
dpa Fotoreport, Frankfurt/Main S. 18/Stoppelmann/Koch, 58/Mahnke, 61/Scheidemann,
Environmental Images, London S. 75/McCarthy
Cornelia Federn-Ronacher, Berlin S. 36
David Graham Picturefile, London S. 85 (3)
IFA-Bilderteam, Düsseldorf S. 27/Arakaki
IMAGE BANK, Berlin S. 7/Hussey & Hussey
Helga Lade Fotoagentur, Berlin S. 18/MAN
Rainer Lang, Berlin S. 38
NEWS Team International Ltd., Birmingham S. 34, 35
Premium Stock Photography, Düsseldorf S. 9/Images, 20/Images
Jeffrey Tabberner, Oxford S. 40, 71 (4)
The Stock Market, Düsseldorf S. 17/Prezant, 21/Keller
Tony Stone Bilderwelten, Hamburg S. 7/Heleotis, 16/Cohen, 24/Heleotis, 30/Pollok, 38/Bushnell & Soifer, 44/Coppock, 45/Latham, 56/Jons, 59/Talbot/Torres/Sacks/Condit II, 60/Rusing, 75/Allison, 76/Hodges, 77/Pickerell
Wildlife, Hamburg S. 95/Shah/Jones/Mallwitz/Kenney
Peter Wirtz, Dormagen S. 68
ZEFA-Zentrale Farbbild Agentur, Düsseldorf S. 27/Boschung, 28/Index Stock, 68/Benser/Schlotmann,

Grafiken/Cartoons:
Oxprint, Oxford S. 6, 14, 31/Ed McLachlan, S. 48, 91, 93/Corinne Burrows, S. 51/Oxford Illustrators, S. 66/Ian Lewis, S. 78, 87/Oxprint Design, S. 79/Graham-Cameron Illustration, S. 89/David Mostyn

Songtext:
Another Day in Paradise (S. 38) M./T.: Phil Collins
© 1989 by Phil Collins Ltd./Hit & Run Music (Publ) Ltd.
Alle Rechte bei Edition Hitrunner c/o Neue Welt Musikverlag GmbH, München

Wir danken für die freundliche Unterstützung:
Careers and Occupational Centre, Sheffield; MIZZ Magazine, IPC Young Women's Group, London; Oxy, GB; Spillers Foods International (Choosy), Surrey

Nicht alle Copyright-Inhaber konnten ermittelt werden; deren Urheberrechte werden hiermit vorsorglich und ausdrücklich anerkannt.